MW00980097

Changes

Clearing the Atmosphere

Nature is not simply a technological
or economical resource, and human beings
are not mere numbers. To suggest that one
can somehow align all the squabbling institutions
of science, environmental management, government
and diplomacy in an alliance of convenience
to regulate the global climate seems
to be optimistic.

James Buchan

Linda Varsell Smith

Acknowledgments

Artistic Climate Changer

Maureen Therrien Frank
Formatter and Illustrator
TheMandalaLady.com

Climate Information

Copyright © 2020
ISPN: 978-1-716-48945-7

Rainbow Communications
461 NW Hemlock Ave.
Corvallis, OR 97330

varsell4@comcast.net.

Poet Climate Changer

Linda Varsell Smith

Born in New Britain, Connecticut, Linda now lives in Corvallis, Oregon. She has also lived in Washington, Virginia, Maryland, Massachusetts and Arizona. She has traveled to Europe, but for over 50 years calls Oregon home. Linda is a retired teacher of creative writing in workshops and at a local community college. She was an editor at Calyx Books for over 30 years and served as president of the Oregon Poetry Association. She is currently president of PEN Women in Portland. She belongs to several poetry and writer's critique groups and is part of Writing the Wrongs to Rights Huddle. She is an avid cooperative and competitive Scrabble player. Linda appreciates plays, poetry readings, science and arts. She lives among over 3000 angels and seasonal miniatures with her husband Court. She likes to escape quarantine in her backyard, to gather chi.

Climates Contents

Weather Climate

Changes in Climate

Complex Climate

Emotional Climate

Social Climate

Political Climate

Spiritual Climate

Future Climate

Cosmic Climates

Climate of Uncertainty

Weather Climate

Climate is what we expect,
weather is what we get.

Mark Twain

Gray Skies

Gray skies scowling at me
nothing but gray skies do I see...
It is three o'clock, decision time.

My husband's home from a bike ride.
I have staffed the phone. Now he showers
to rid himself of world's detritus.

I sit with lap blanket facing the damp
chilly backyard behind glass.
The morning sun has vanished.

I waited too long to go out. Now
I can see a blue jay grub the garden
way apart from even social distance.

When a peephole of sun splays
a faint shadow across the lawn,
I am briefly hopeful if I wait, maybe...

At least a few jays flyby, a rustle
of tiny brown birds in the bushes.
Most movement is wimpy from pinwheel,

limp wind-chimes, stagnant yard angels.
The gaps in the leaning wooden back fence
droop more visible. We do not own it to fix.

I await updates on friends and family
facing various health and financial challenges.
I'm stuck inside and unable to visit them.

I was really hoping the morning blue skies
would last longer. Tomorrow, whenever
the sun appears, I'm venturing outside.

I'll lasso some chi, chuff my chakras,
send hopeful vibes into the universe.
Until then, I'll high-five and fingerprint glass.

Rainbow Weather

Gloomy gray then radiant
sun. Rains then dries up.
Defiant.

Layers of clothes go on and off.
Outdoors is a crap shoot.
Gag and cough.

Air quality: fog or clear.
We must clean up our
atmosphere.

Rainbow in the sky—
joy supply.

Rainbow Magic.

Rained all
night and most
of today. Two rainbows
swished in sky magically on our
way home.

The sky
had patches of
blue amid the cloudy
turbulent gray, so dark, heavy
laden.

Seeing
rainbows sparked our
spirits. Dark sunglasses
enhanced the dazzling, luminous
colors.

We searched
for patches of
rainbows poking through gray.
Sun blinking in and out, makes view
vibrant.

We go
inside with bright
images of delight.
Carry two rainbows for our minds
and hearts.

Retreating

Downpours
to showers to
mizzle, rain still drizzles.
Raingear stocked, ready for use
in car.

I watch
through windows.
Rain dribbles down the glass.
Recently set record water
drenching.

Good day
for a long nap
under warm covers or
gaze through streaking windows, feet up
on couch

When sun
brings rainbows we
are dazzled by winter
color swishing peek-a-boos in
the sky.

January in Willamette Valley Oregon

water gushes from
roof gutters road gutters flow
mini-streams   babble

holiday decorations
slow to take down in cold rain
try before the snow

blue candles in windows
blue lights rim the front door
starry light grounded

foggy, cloudy days
smoggy, cloggy, rainfall
beats forest fires

scrawny bare branches
silhouettes or shadows etch
heavy gray skies

Winter Storm

Tree fell,
knocking out a
power line briefly, as
power company revived the
punched line.

Power
out a while, so
I took a nap while poor
wind-writhing branches blew leaves left.
Birds flown.

Rain, snow,
glints of sun as
strong winds push over
garbage cans, then they roll into
the street.

Drivers
afraid of snow,
icy streets and blocked roads.
Weather changes hourly through
the day.

Some schools
and meetings are
cancelled. I cocoon warm
at home. Some brave gray dim-lit skies–
some not.

Sidewalks
slippery some
times, depends on how cold.
Walkers and bikers guess slick lanes
and dare.

Weather
predicted not
punctual. We're flummoxed.
How many and who can come from
how far?

Light's on.
Heater pumping.
Screens and digital lights
ready to greet chilled guests and
my words.

Mid-January Feasting

Hungry
birds peck front yard,
bustle about in light,
snow-powdered grass and on snow-crusted
stone wall.

Robins,
stellar jays and
little brown jobbers feast
on holly berries and stand on
cold feet.

Wildlife
sculptures lined up
under windows witness
the tussle. More grass appears as
snow melts.

Where were
the birds as it
snowed? Sheltered in bird
houses? Under bushes, porches?
Compost?

Why did
they stay so late?
Not fair-weather friends? One
flock swarmed with no fly pattern
like geese.

Soon snow
melts. Grass green and
open. Fog lifted. They leave.
Finally decide it's time to
head south?

Stellar Jay Amid Holly

As the
fog lifts, a jay
perches on holly branch,
no hurry to feast, fluffing its
feathers.

Jay seems
to see me, but
the window shields us from
contact. This bird does not attack
window.

Unlike
the visitor
who banged-head at bush's
reflection, this bird hangs on branch
tightly.

We sit
and stare, wonder
what each other perceives,
see who stares the longest. Focus
human!

The bird
has enough of
such nonsense and flies off.
Holly berries safe for day with
no birds?

Window
basks in sun, shines
undisturbed on this Earth patch.
Sun stokes Australian fires,
scorches land.

The jay
has local threats,
but in my front yard some
respite from danger, lingering
in peace.

Staying Put

Sometimes I just want to stay home.
despite the weather outside,
use my energy to write a poem
with a space heater at my side,
Or snuggled in bed for a nap,
sometimes heating pad, shoulder, lap.

Despite the weather outside
even if it is warm and sunny,
I'd rather relax, think, besides
I'm retired from making money.
So why not do what I want to do,
devote time and energy as I want to?

Use my energy to write a poem
is my favorite preoccupation.
Any chance to create is welcome,
is a priority over a distracting occasion.
I can be immobile yet free,
exploring my creativity.

With a space heater at my side,
when the room feels chilly and drafty,
I can take my surroundings in stride
and remain productively crafty.
Just me and the keys, some dark chocolate,
water, light, quiet and I can create.

Or snuggled in bed for a nap
sometimes I sleep or compose
lines for a poem or perhaps
some ideas I'd like to propose.
Thinking or dreaming ideas appear
to ponder and to try to make clear

Sometimes heating pad, shoulder, lap,
liver, knees, lower back— wherever required
to ease pain, get back to word-play in a snap,
to try to gain the results I desired.
Staying put is a satisfying venture.
I go outside for adventure.

Leaf-Shine

The leaves sparkle in spring sun.
Grass briskly prickles with dew.
Rain drains the clouds, brings greening.

Inside peeking outside, the window
frames outlook like mosaics.
Cataract clearing eyes intensify colors.

In our yard, things are pretty tranquil
in a worrying world. A place of sanctuary.
A place to gather warmth, energize from chi.

It is not quite warm enough to sit outside,
but inside I can get inspired to create
and hope, watch leaf-shine heralding spring.

Tree Advocate

Arborists arrived today.
Balancing a lop-sided job?
The truck parked in my way.
How many branches will they lob?
        I love to sit among the trees,
        to watch the birds and the breeze.

Balancing a lop-sided job?
The last attempt was painful to see.
How many limbs will they knob?
Some beyond repair unfortunately.
        A tall spruce cut up above power line.
        Below naked rounds. Ugly design.

The truck parked in my way.
They had to move it to let me out.
I fretted while I was away.
I didn't want arborists about.
        The last attempt by a clueless crew
        did not seem to know what to do.

How many branches will they lob?
It's winter so I can easily tell.
If I look will I once again sob?
Wait for spring when leaves cover well?
        So far I can't face the yard.
        Last trimming cut me hard.

I love to sit among the trees,
breathe deep and draw in chi,
daydream among their canopies
sustained by their beauty.
        But last year they were whacked.
        My serenity was attacked.

To watch the birds and the trees.
seated in a blue-pillowed chair,
I encourage dandelions and bees,
appreciate nature's expressions there.
        It may be a few weeks
        before I brave a few peeks.

Puny Peachy Payoff

Husband
took from puny
peach branch, to hide in some
nearby rhododendrons a small
sensor

for his
electronics.
The tree produced one peach.
Perhaps, now unloaded it will
produce.

Diseased
cherry tree chopped
down was once abundant.
Will the peach tree revive the will
to thrive?

Peach tree
now more fertile?
Loss of electrical
pulse, can tree revive for peachy
payoff?

Gazing at the Backyard Trees

Looking out the window
from the sun room
in the February chill, the trees

just trimmed by an arborist,
strut their showy stuff— fringy
at tips of branches, but balanced

from the lopsided, whack job of their
previous arborist encounter. I mourn
the circular wounds and ringed scars.

The apple and hazelnut limbs
are higher off the ground and canopies
reach, a little less straggly, skyward.

The lawn, so lush and green,
showcases the new arboreal
make overs. The tree-tips lacy.

The poor peach was left alone
with spindly branches and limp
stoop. Too ill to heal more wounds.

Pear and plum trees are out of my
sight, so I'll check them out
in the spring when I join the trees

to loop chi, earth core to cosmos
(theoretically) to heal and connect
with All in my blue-pillowed chair.

In a month or so I can sit among
the trees, the metal and concrete angels,
sniff the flowers and observe wildlife.

I will have had cataracts removed from
both eyes and may see details clearly,
not blurry. I will breathe in chi from warmer air.

I am anxious to rejoin these shadow-makers,
to stimulate all my senses, to gaze in delight
at the refurbished, healing trees.

This Week's Entry: Ending 2/21/20
Earthweek: Diary of a Changing World. Steve Newman

This week
ice volcanoes
expand ice shelf of Lake
Michigan in frigid blast from
the north.

Earthquakes
in Persian Gulf,
Papua, New Guinea,
Malulu Islands, Fiji, east
Taiwan.

Cow burps
get masks to trap
methane, fifteen percent
of greenhouse gas. Masked burps turned to
water.

Insects
get a foothold
in Antarctica. How
did they arrive? Join invasive
crane fly.

Seafood
soup cooked in warm
New Zealand water kills
mussels, clams and cockles. Climate
changes?

Oil and
gas industries
underestimated
methane emissions to greenhouse
gases.

Cyclone
brought heavy rain
to parts of Australia,
New Zealand, damaged heritage
island.

Seeing White
>A spring Sunday contemplating in the backyard.

White blossoms on the plum and pear trees.
Contrail diffuses in a cloud-less sky.
White-breasted bird perches on the power pole.

White stripes blur with blue on the pinwheel.
White butterfly flits across the garden. Finally
some jays skitter white specks in the rhododendrons.

When a white-breasted blue jay briefly lands
on the apple branch right before me, I conjure
my blue-loving mother saying hi from beyond.

White-edged holly leaves, white-shine on
blades of grass, white-gray lichen sprigs
in the lawn. White-splotches on tree trunks

and stone walls. White plastic buckets,
white paint splotches on unpainted board.
Speckles of white appear everywhere.

White temperature regulator unit outside
for inside self-quarantiners. I will go inside
to white walls in comfort.

White helicopter weather station whirls
on fence top of my neighbor, above
white daffodils, gently waving.

My red cape is a stop light in a mostly
go green world. A brown bug lands on a grass
blade before me. My white focus ends.

Unseen the virus and the warming sun
rays soothing my back. Reluctantly, I
leave this whitened world, calmed.

Full Worm Supermoon
    March 8-9th 2020

The Native Americans call
the moon which heralds spring,
the Worm Moon because they recall
the ground softens, earthworms bring
        birds back to feed.
        Moon fulfills a compelling need.

The moon which heralds spring
is when moon closest to earth orbit,
at 90% perigee. Hope no clouds ring
our view or inclement weather so can see it.
        Four supermoons this year.
        We hope our views are clear.

The Worm Moon because they recall
the impact of season's beginning.
Crow Moon, Sap Moon, Sugar Moon not all
the names people find winning.
        Catholics name it Lenten Moon,
        know Lent will be soon.

The ground softens and earthworms bring
signals for seeds and birds to thrive.
The spring equinox has earlier March 19th arriving.
Spring is the season to become alive—
        warming the planet climate change or not.
        memories of blooming, bugs to swat.

Birds back to feed,
uplift spirits and mood.
get ready to nest and breed,
brighten up the neighborhood.
        I watch the winged-ones take flight
        long to fly with them in delight.

Moon fulfills a compelling need,
keeps us and planet in balance,
surveys us destroying ourselves with greed,
probably wonders if humanity will advance.
        Moon is female symbol on International Women's Day.
        Women want gender equality, freedom from abuse–today.

17

First Backyard Excursion

At mid-afternoon on St. Patrick's Day
I don my blue hoodie and mother's red cape
and venture into the verdant backyard.

The cloud-smudged blue sky warms the chill.
The sun on my back also tints my glasses.
The metal chair is without my blue pillow.

Immediately I spy the lavender stalks
in the concrete- chunked wall and larger
lavender blooms peeking through ivy.

The trimmed apple, hazelnut, peach trees
are more balanced, no droopy lower limbs.
Even the stooped peach tree stands taller.

A robin and scrub jay snack side by side
pecking the garden dirt. The jay flies
to the peach tree, which looks like a bird in flight.

As the jay climbs to the peach top, I see
clusters of pink buds. Perhaps the ailing tree
is recovering! So glad it wasn't whacked down.

The angel weathervane may have shifted north,
after months immobile, pointing west. Rusty angel
Airlika, blows her horn at me from a hazelnut limb.

The pinwheel spins vigorously. The wind-chimes
ding jingles robustly. Our neighbors whirligigs
twirl over a batch of white daffodils.

The trees are still encrusted with moss and lichen.
Iris blades greening, but not flowering yet. Same with
rhododendrons and azaleas hugging the fence.

Angel Bottom is still prone on the blue table beside
a metal bluebird companion. I am a new companion
returning to the backyard after a turbulent winter.

After a few deep breathes and looping chi from
the core of the earth to the cosmos, observing
the seasonal changes, soaking in energy,

      I waddle back inside for my self-quarantine,
      after energizing from breathing some fresh air.

On the Spring Equinox

A cloudless bluetiful sky on this early
Spring Equinox, frames the backyard
where I have come to slurp some chi.

A puffball, beside a more youthful
companion, promises a proliferation
of my beloved dandelions to freckle the grass.

On the top of the apple tree white buds
sprout above nubbins on the lower-lying
limbs. Hazelnut trees' buds await blooming.

Nearby a neighbor's noisy, munching machine
rumbles and grumbles over something,
disturbs the quiet, mutes the wind chimes.

No-see-um airplanes resound without contrails.
Blue jays and brown birds huddle near the wooden
back fence, held upright by slanted wood planks.

Birds skirmish amid the bushes and peck ground.
Some snack on an apple branch, but mostly hunker near
the stone wall of the higher garden–solo, with little interaction.

Tootsie, the weathervane angel refuses
to budge. The pinwheel spins erratically.
Above me, dangling angel Airlika pirouettes.

I am determined to wait out the machine
and have a few moments of peace and quiet
before heading inside. It is a long wait.

I try to tune out the noise and focus on visual
cues and contemplation, breathing with life around
me, calming my anxiety until distraction ends.

The warming sun urges me to stay, but I push my
walker over to the back door, greet rain-washed, prone
Bottom angel who still holds a yellow, mini-ball on his feet.

April Fools Day

Weathercasters predicted sun to appear
around four. No joke. It did, prompting
my husband's daily bike ride.

Incessant rain is hail in some places.
It is too cold for me to venture from
beyond the wall of windows.

My daily vigil is performed without
my red cape or shoes. But an afghan
with loopy holes covers my legs.

Sharp dark shadows yawn across
uniformly mowed boring lawn.
No remnants of dandelions.

He insists on manicuring the yards.
The front yard has abundant dandelions.
They migrate sparsely to the backyard.

No one but us has been in the backyard
in months. Since we switched to electric,
not even a gas meter reader. It's capped.

Shadows fade with fickle clouds.
Pinwheel's and wind-chimes' tempo
changes at whim of the wind.

We are self-quarantining. I welcome
seeing waves of freedom, wildness.
Not a fan of clipping nature.

He is proud of his handiwork. I am annoyed.
But why should I whine when the unruly,
traumatic world is just out of sight–suffering?

My solace is chilled, darkened, dampened.
How long must I soul-dig inside? They insist
we will get through this together. How or when?

Five O'Clock Shadow

Between rain bursts, the sun
casts a 5:00 shadow across
the green stubble of the backyard.

I am exercising my birthday privilege
to view the scene through two rows
of glass, past a shaded enclosed room.

I have my red cape and lap quilt.
I am dry and warm as I peruse
the framed darkening landscape.

Dandelions shelter in place within
their seeds. Those who burst free
of lock down, social distance across lawn.

Wind-wriggling, spindly hazelnut limbs
sway rusty, angel Airlika who honks
her hollow horn over my empty chair.

Tootsie, the weathervane angel
stolidly toots her slender horn northwest
beside our occasionally agitated pinwheel.

The wind chimes clang loudly when
provoked. Then I spot a yellow spark
on the back fence. My husband does not see it.

He reports a neighbor's backyard light
might sparkle between the fence slats.
I'll conjure an angel's flashlight.

I keep looking for birds. Can't see any
creatures lurking in the bushes or trees.
Too early for dinner, too late for snacks?

The shadows stretch East. I cannot see
the whole picture sitting inside. I doubt
I'd see the whole picture anywhere.

A global chill is keeping us shut-in. Breaths
of fresh, healthy air–treasured. I relish phone,
paper and on-line contacts until we can touch.

Lull in Storms

Mid-afternoon in a lull between
storms, my husband risks a bike ride.
I stay inside and observe the backyard.

Through glass, in filtered air, the
lull brings the backyard to a standstill.
No wind-chime jingle or pinwheel spin.

A steady stream of rain dribbles from
the gutter outside the back door. The yard
is drenched. I'll cuddle in my red cape inside.

No birds flyover or land in the mossy branches.
Rusty angel Airlika dangles from the hazelnut
limb, pointing at my empty, cold, wet, black chair.

Bottom, the prone concrete angel is taking
a bath in his blue table tub. Tootsie, the angel
weathervane is oblivious to wind.

I strain to check up on dandelions, but they
seem in remission. Lupin look lush and
white blossoms on the pear tree— profuse.

I hear the rain on the skylight, but the biker
appears undeterred from his hour trek. I
deferred my backyard chi time–deep breathe.

I sigh. Exhale sadness and inhale hope,
pretend self-quarantine is a staycation.
The wet biker returns, refreshed and safe.

Changes in Climate

Look at climate change. Understand
that it is going to have a profound effect
on our resources and so much else.

Hillary Clinton

Counteracting Climate Change

Climate change is not a problem that can be solved or mitigated enough by individual behavior, though it is good, important and a place to start. Tatiana Schlossberg

Reading all the statistics can be overwhelming
making us feel the challenge is too hard to fix.
Each minuscule role of an individual
must be added into the global mix.

We can't all do everything.
This must be a unified effort,
but we can make helpful changes
which can bring added support.

Each sustainable action can help.
Awareness needs to broaden our scope.
Without humanity our planet could recover.
Meanwhile we must find ways to cope.

Unless planet is whacked by cosmic blow,
Earth should survive our blundering.
Will we be part of the solution?
Many folks are wondering.

Weather extremes, species extinctions,
melting glaciers calve icebergs into the sea.
Fires burn, migrations and displacements,
polluted Earth needs our attention urgently.

Trying to Remain Human

Being a human these days–
takes a heavy toll on body and soul.
We search for actions we can praise.
We struggle to remain whole.
> Extremes impinge on our center.
> So much room for despair to enter.

Takes a heavy toll on body and soul
to breathe polluted air, befouled climate.
Our spirit reaches out to play a role
the planet will appreciate.
> Just being a fleshy, bio-being
> today it's risky from the mischief I'm seeing.

We search for actions we can praise,
for leadership to meet challenges— just
make changes so our well-being will raise
with other creatures with integrity and trust.
> Are humans too numerous, too defective
> to cooperate and be effective?

We struggle to remain whole
as our resources continue to shrink.
Is any type of survival our goal?
Can we achieve a global re-think?
> Are conditions so dank and dire
> we can't achieve what we desire?

Extremes impinge on our center
gnaw at our consciousness until raw.
We wait for hope and trust to re-enter.
Some core, some chart, some light to draw.
> when things appear dark and lost
> and we're facing a holocaust.

So much room for despair to enter
What is the universe decreeing?
Re-seeding? The arrival of a mentor?
Any future predicted worth seeing?
> Extinction caused by us or an intervention?
> I wonder what would be the intention?

Nuclear Winter

If even small nuclear
blast set loose- we'll see
winter near.

Soot cools atmosphere, crops fail,
ocean food chain cut,
species bail.

Climate crisis enough to
try to handle, now
not wars too.

Nowhere for covers.
Death hovers.

A New Outlook

Change is
not the end, it
is the beginning of
a new cycle— it's a better
outlook.

Focus
on the good we
see coming to help us
be part of planet's renewal
and us.

When we
despair the light's
dim and snuffs out.
Adapt, assist, cope, believe best–
the way.

I'll need
a flashlight in
the dark, sunglasses
by day to keep shining when I
feel lost.

I'll greet
new decade by
opening doors and hearts,
letting go of old ideas.
heal, dare.

I won't
be stuck in past.
I'll free myself to be
advocate for humanity
and Earth.

At least
I'll try my best
to hope and act kindly,
change to begin a new cycle,
prevail.

Smoke Circling the World

The Australian fires have come full circuit
around the globe–smoke everywhere.
No matter what your point of view of it,
climate change says we must prepare.
        Such devastation on such a large scale.
        Then add plastic pollution to the tale.

Around the globe– smoke everywhere.
Local pollution adds to the toll.
Hard to breath in toxic air.
We are not performing steward's role.
        Australia serves as sentinel
        the planet is not doing well.

No matter what your point of view of it
it is difficult to deny we face dire times.
It does not take much to intuit
there's droughts and floods in some climes.
        We are facing weather extremes.
        It is as dangerous as it seems.

Climate change says we must prepare
to mitigate the future impact.
First we must make people aware,
learn what is scientific fact.
        What can we do as an individual?
        Act on what is actual.

Such devastation on such a large scale
effects all species and forms of life.
Billions of beings will not prevail.
We face many aspects of strife.
        Can we find enough solutions
        and the needed resolutions?

Then add plastics to the tale.
Soon more plastics in sea than fish.
Plastic in everything, scientists detail
of micro-bits. Ban plastics–I wish.
        It is hard to remain hopeful, have a voice.
        Can we do it? Do we have any choice?

Some Like It Hotter?

> *Scientists calculate to reach this temperature oceans have taken in 228 sextillian jules, about 3.6 billion times the amount of heat released by the Hiroshima bombings.* Simina Mistreanu

The last
decade was the
hottest on record. More
than ninety percent went into
the sea.

Less than
four percent went
into the land, and the
atmosphere since 1970.
Sea sweats.

Instead
of brisk sea dip,
soon we'll go there to bathe?
People can work to reverse our
impact.

Past six
decades warming
increased 450%
percent. Major increase is changed
climate.

Sea-swim
with plastic mess,
gunk up nets and leave them.
Glaciers calve, coastlines flood, dry air
brings drought.

More heat
not always best.
Can we adapt? In time?
Mass extinctions happened before.
Again?

Cancer Alleys

Gas and fossil fuels plants
often shift to making plastics
and petrochemicals to pollute
the air and kill us.

St James Parish in Mississippi
is fighting another lethal plant
from Taiwan. They already live
in Cancer Alley, also called "death row".

When we can make biodegradable plastics
from sustainable seaweed and need to ban
fossil fuels, coal— all the major polluters
to our environment, why do we bring in more?

Anywhere these pesticides and other
nasty plants exist they create Cancer
Alleys where cancer rates skyrocket
in pockets of poverty and amid minorities.

The ones who create the most pollution
impact the poor who contribute the least.
Environmental injustice and disempowerment,
we must change our life styles.

Poisoning land, water and air makes
viability and sustainability difficult.
There is a cancer on our souls. No one
will escape the consequences of inaction.

Polluted Paradise

Broken
sewage system
brings toxic floods flowing
over Fort Lauderdale. Tourists stay
away.

Smells with
waste, diseased
waterways polluted.
Repairs could take years to clean the
water.

Noah's
big flood had ark.
Too many now to board.
The horde could perish, from planet.
Extinct.

What can
we control, repair?
Do we have the time or
the will, or ideas to then
survive?

Phase Out Chlorpyrifos in Oregon–Everywhere

Chlorpyrifos should be banned to protect
farmworkers from the pesticide and eaters
of strawberries, broccoli, lettuce and other crops.

Chlorpyrifos was developed in WWII
as a chemical weapon. As a pesticide
it is now killing our own civilians.

Chlorpyrifos causes diseases like cancer,
causes miscarriages, brain tumors, ADHD,
developmental delays, autism and more.

Chlorpyrifos clings to farmworkers' clothes
and endangers their families. Oregon must pass
Healthy Kids and Farmworkers Act.

Chlorpyrifos legislation passed in Hawaii,
California, New York and European Union.
We must phase out–at least— and ban it.

Chlorpyrifos endangers us all. I did not
even know about it. I do not like strawberries,
lettuce or broccoli. Now I am glad I don't.

Purposeful Walking

Because
my mother did
not drive, I had to walk
home for lunch, to library. They're
long walks.

Also
alone at times.
Today I would not let
my child walk along a major
roadway.

Times have
changed, we felt safe.
If with a friend we liked
to chat when weather was good, but
sometimes,

cold, wet,
miserable
walk. When Mrs. Greening drove
we really appreciated
the ride.

No bus
to school until
high school. Boys flicked frog eyes
at girls. Unpleasant jaunt to school
until

boyfriend
drove me to school.
We dated through high school.
I had rides everywhere I wished.
Broke up.

I had
license to drive
but Dad had the car for
work and he drove me to local
college.

Our kids
rode buses or
schools close walk with others,
but both parents would drive if we're
needed.

On the Wagon

...alcohol production and distribution can be quite energy intensive. So what if you want to reduce your environmental footprint, but you're not quite ready to hop on the wagon and stay there? Miranda Green

To join the green climate bandwagon,
you might consider staying on the wagon.
Drinkers get more mileage out of liquor
for a buzz and greener— "Liquor is quicker".

Wine and beer cause more emissions
of greenhouse gas. Higher transmissions.
One six-pack of beer emits the same
as driving a car eight miles in the green game.

Larger beer emissions come from refrigeration
and production and transport are considerations.
Packing materials enter the equations.
Cans best, can be recycled, in many situations.

Shipping distance is another cost. Vats come by sea.
West coast from Pacific. East coast from Atlantic can be
best for the environment. Read labels to know
products' origins and how far it had to go.

So if you drink, drink responsibly.
It's not all about you, you see.
So I'll remain an abstainer,
try to be a better sustainer.

Clogging Carbon Sinks

Carbon
sinks are losing
their ability to suck
CO2 and are in peril,
as well.

We must
do more. Protect
our hope for surviving
climate changes that endanger
us all.

The news
is grim as we
exploit our forests and
increase pollution in our air
and land.

Waste clogs
our oceans. Where
will carbon sink? Plastic
micro-bits in animals, also
humans.

Leaders
must change outlook
and act sustainably.
Saving our trees is good bet to
survive?

Other
sources can kill
us off, but we create
our extinction. Destructive
stewards?

Lure of the Wild and Nurtured

Outside
I draw some chi
in my backyard, watch trees,
gardens, wild animals display
their gifts.

I sit
when it's sunny
and hopefully warm, breathe
deeply color, texture, living
beings,

re-wild
in my mind what
was here before people
claimed dominance, exploited
others.

We are
organic. We
nourish what we can with
no pesticides to poison or
threaten.

Whether
wild or nurtured,
life can flourish freely.
I keep watch to learn, also be
nourished.

Be for the Bees

Be
for
the bees
as many
die-off. Millions
in recent years. Increasing.

Bees
need
more safe
habitat.
Toxic pesticides,
vegetation loss culprits.

Roads,
crop,
fields and
neighborhoods
disrupt food, nesting
sites critical to survival.

We
have
room. We're
organic
I love dandelions.
Some states have laws to protect bees.

We
can
ban the
pesticides
that kill bees and stop
bee-killing, promote awareness.

Save
these
special,
important,
pollinators who
bring forth beauty, our nourishment.

Haiku- holly

birds sprinkle holly
tree lured by leaf-shine and hope
for berries return

New Zealand's Tree of Hope

Submerged
Wanaka tree
in Lake Wanaka was
vandalized, lower limb sawed, hope
symbol.

Lone tree,
a Crack Willow.
Roots in shallow water.
UNESCO World Heritage Site
damaged.

Taiki
promise, asked of
visitors, requests them to
be stewards of environment.
Most are.

Southern Alps
frame lake and tree.
Picturesque lower limb
gone. Photographers grieve destroyed
image.

Kea,
alpine parrot
in the Alps endangered
as well by destructive, evil
tourists?

Tragic
nature assaults
diminish beauty and our
survival. The weeping willow
is mourned.

World Pangolin Day

Valentine's Day attention turns
to the pangolin's plight.
Illegal trade in pangolin products
caused 195,000 deaths last year despite

an international ban on all trade
of pangolins by traffickers worldwide.
Poachers in Asia and Africa sell pangolin
parts on Internet. See populations slide.

All eight species are endangered
and protected by international wildlife law.
Their scales and meat are eaten, used in meds
and leather products, prized by outlaw.

Now they are blamed for coronavirus.
This might diminish their appeal.
All illegal wildlife or legal too
should not be killed. Find a new deal.

March 1st 2020

Climate
change with early
whales, seed, buds, blooms and bird
migrations bring the early spring
greening.

Trees blast—
flowering plums,
dogwoods swish with color.
Daffodils, forsythia, and
crocus.

China's
viral attacks
shuts down air pollution
as quarantines cities, people,
their jobs

In the
radio news
on bleak economy.
Natural disasters persist,
destroy.

When it
is warmer, I'll
go to the backyard to
seek greening, deep breathing, solace,
and chi.

For now
until vision
clears I try to stay safe,
cope and hope, play and rest the best
I can.

Gently Falls the Rain

The Earth is quieter and less polluted
due to less emissions from shut down
people, staying in place.

In the wild west we are taming our
excessive appetites, but the crazy
eight mid-west states remain unbridled.

I ramble around my disbanded corona coven,
sit inside the glass door with its row of sunflowers
to remind people it is there and to ponder exiting.

When we had more grubby hands about,
fingerprints imprinted the glass, but now
we are to wash our hands. Notice sunflowers.

I am noticing dandelions to celebrate them
tomorrow on their special day. In the front
yard they are social-distancing gracefully.

In the backyard I spy four low-lying blooms
and two hugging the stone wall. Not too many
to compose dandy-lines in their honor.

It is a rainy, chilly, late spring. Few birds stay
to snack, most stay briefly to catch their breath.
More birds perch and peck in more abundant yards.

The rain gently falls, almost invisible. The yard
angels, pinwheel, wind-chimes are still. We
all wait a cleansing breeze to breathe safely.

Complex Climate

I don't think we're evolved to the point
we're clever enough to handle as complex
a situation as climate change. The inertia
of humans is so huge that you can't
really do anything meaningful.

James Lovelock

Interrobang

Punctuation mark used in various written languages and intended to combine the functions of the question mark or interrogative point and the exclamation mark or exclamation point, known in the jargon of printers and programmers as a "bang". The glyph is the superimposition of these two points. The interrobang was first proposed in the 1960s by Martin K. Speckter.   Internet definition

Now time of interrobang
global condition—
our "big bang."

Emphatic questions arise.
Answers not solved.
No surprise.

Interrobang used in forceful
communication—
resourceful.

You want things to shift?
Use the glyph.

Seeking New Leadership

Churches, temples, mosques and synagogues
have been targets for hate by terrorists.
Faithful and non-faithful act violently
against diverse interpretations of how to live.

Add sexism, racism, bigotry, intolerance, violence
and humanity is just a diverse, perverse mess.
We seek community with like-minded people,
but we don't have to exclude others or accept their views.

After all the division, maltreatment, humanity
can't seem to get along, stop bullying.
Even our festivals of light dim as a new year
begins and we retreat to our old ways.

I saw a picture of 90,000 Jews celebrating
Daf Yomi, a seven year cycle of reading
the Talmud one page a day. All pictured were men.
Hierarchy of most religions are men.

Horrific rituals are performed on women in the name
of traditions related to religion. Many women are not
empowered, many of their roles limited to breeders
and households nurturing future abusers.

As the planet's future is in peril. It is the Greta's
and Malala's, #MeToo activists, enlightened
leadership we need to wake up men who could
cause the demise of many forms of life.

Focusing on the World

*By focusing our attention on this world, all of us together–and I mean every
person, every animal, plant, mineral and energetic spirit–forms an image we call
this world regardless of our perspective.* Will Bradley.

No matter how we view the world we are
all connected, despite all the divisions.
We are all descended from a star.
No matter if we have different visions.
>We are all on a personal quest
>to understand ourselves and all the rest.

All connected, despite all the divisions.
We all face a possible dimensional shift.
For Gaia's sake we must make re-visions
if we are to make this lighter uplift.
>How will we preserve our planet's survival?
>Do we have to await for another revival?

We are all descended from a star—
stardust to stardust during this life.
Must we imagine a cosmic avatar
to lead us out of our fear and strife?
>Humanity is on the brink
>and faces extinction, I think.

No matter if we have different visions
somehow we must choose love over hate.
Will we make the proper provisions
to wake up and participate?
>We are destroying the planet's viability
>by our lack of taking responsibility.

We are all on a personal quest
to determine our mission, unlock our code.
It is urgent we do our best
to be open to any light-filled download.
>We tend to be ego prone.
>We cannot succeed if act alone.

To understand ourselves and all the rest
demands we unleash our soul-power.
To the future, what will we bequest?
What actions will we empower?
>Despite fulfilling all our intentions,
>we might not be welcome in other dimensions.

Quid pro quo? Status quo?

When the Earth was seeded
was it quid pro quo–what with whom?
Was it done because life was needed?
To replenish the status quo?
        A new experiment to master?
        To recover from disaster?

Was it quid pro quo–what with whom?
Our destiny part of a cosmic plan?
Become a new species to bloom?
What did we exchange to become human?
        Who set up this arrangement?
        Tossed off by estrangement?

Was it done because life was needed
to be Gaia's companions and stewards?
Were any precautions to be heeded?
Any instructions to be moving towards?
        Abandoned to try free will?
        Sounds like we have limitations still.

To replenish the status quo?
A civilization destroyed by extinction?
Can we learn what we must know?
What will be our path and distinction?
        If the only constant is change, perhaps
        we are experiencing a relapse?

A new experiment to master?
A chance to try again?
Some have become a doom forecaster,
question the need for such stress and pain.
        Some ask about our mission here.
        The answers are far from clear.

To recover from disaster
means we should become sustainable.
Must we work much faster?
Each contribute what one is able?
        Our energy and consciousness
        can get us out of this mess?

Awaiting Good News

According to numerology, 2020—
a #4 year, a builder of grounded
manifestation, a year of plenty.
Actions on which the decade is founded.
        I am not a fan of numbers really.
        However I yearn for hope ideally.

A #4 year, a builder of grounded
possibilities to build the life you want.
The call for creativity, inspiration sounded.
Manifest what you feel is important.
        Everything on planet built on energy of 4?
        Shackles off, delays behind us–free once more?

Manifestation, a year of plenty,
of change, freedom, variety,
can appear apparently,
for the planet and society.
        The universe is waiting to solidify
        into reality what matters to you. All qualify?

Actions on which the decade is founded
if commanded for good not dark side
bring happiness, well-being and dreams compounded.
Repel negativity or harmful from touching you, decide
        to become more empowered, enlightened,
        engaged and become less frightened.

I am not a fan of numbers really
but who is to say letters
will bring a more positive reality,
predict more accurately or better.
        I am not sure what is in control.
        Is anyone guiding or on patrol?

However I yearn for hope ideally
to shine our souls for a brighter existence.
Illusion, multi-dimensions, surreality
whatever we experience, provide resistance,
        choose light despite the odds.
        Don't rely on leaders or gods?

Imponderabilia

imponderables: things that cannot be precisely determined, measured, or evaluated, the imponderabilia surrounding human life. Dictionary Word of the Day

A wonderful word for the unknown,
perhaps unknowable if life's an illusion.
Cosmic rules and plans ever shown?
Any topics where we've drawn a conclusion?
      Much of existence seems based on guesses.
      Our mistakes can make colossal messes.

Perhaps unknowable if life's an illusion.
I'm perhaps a controlled hologram?
Any junctures of multi-dimensional fusion?
I'm surely confused about who I am.
      It seems humanity is on trial.
      Are we to be lead by denial?

Cosmic rules and plans ever shown?
Coded within our DNA?
What insights should we hone?
Try to cope, come what may?
      Goals and time-lines don't always align.
      Perhaps in my destiny or not mine?

Any topics where we've drawn a conclusion?
Certainly not climate change or even if Earth flat?
Some rely on consensus or faith for inclusion,
deny need for a sustainable habitat.
      Where can we turn for guidance?
      Any facts or actions where we have confidence?

Much of existence seems based on guesses
Humanity appears easily deluded,
fickle about what impresses.
Will our presence on Earth be concluded?
      We are all connected, share our fate.
      Why can't we work together and cooperate?

Our mistakes can make colossal messes.
Are we in a state of emergency?
Can we renew and overthrow what oppresses?
Many feel a sense of urgency.
      Imponderabilia surrounds us.
      Can we find a path that grounds us?

Indigenous People

In some remote places
live some indigenous races
unaware what humanity faces.

Just think as your group sustains,
greedy outsiders try to take the reins,
steal the resources your group maintains.

Perhaps these groups are unaware
of the threats and can't prepare
for the devastation coming there.

If preserves protect their cultures
they still could be prey of vultures
breaking treaties by mining, agricultures.

We've learned ancient wisdom from these groups,
discovered plants used in cures, as time interloops.
Some stay with old ways, disregard current bloops.

Just imagine we become extinct.
They never knew what these predators think
and all is gone. We've crossed over the brink.

Lead to Life

Serotiny: process of seeds using the destructive power of fire to trigger germination of new growth.

On the 50th anniversary of Martin Luther King's assassination,
a group called Lead to Life held a ceremony in Atlanta,
to honor life and victims of gun violence.

Weapons of killing were put through fire to forge shovels
and used to plant trees to honor those lost lives. Shovels
assist serotiny and are used in a ceremony to renew and heal.

Shovels can dig up to bury or bring plant life. Guns just kill.
They hope to decompose violence and free life. Shovels
dig for fruit trees, add ashes, soil from violent places.

They hope to heal, learn, and shift together. They listen to mothers
of youth gunned down. I was always glad our son did not
die in war or by guns. Maybe the truck should become shovels.

Ashes radiate youths' energy back to this world. We buried our
son's ashes beside a young tree. The pain lingers. The path
to laughter, health and connection continues for loved ones.

As the arctic, Australia, the Amazon burn and we go down
the alphabet of fire destruction, can the seeds germinate
and restore species lost? Guns to shovels a start.

Shovels tamp fires, plant seed. What do guns contribute?
A world-wide weapons ban could prevent many tragedies.
The world ends in fire or ice? Looks like ice is melting.

Scanning the Internet

There is a LSU mound perhaps
11,300 years old like Gobekli Tepe
much older than Stonehenge and Pyramids.
Maybe among oldest sites found.

Enceladus, moon of Saturn spouts water
with organic compounds, maybe possible life?
Five types of sharks can walk on fins?
Each day more assumptions shattered.

Prophesies about what 02022020 can bring.
On-line courses costing hundreds of dollars
to enlighten you. Health info to scam you.
Little seems impossible these days.

2020 starts with impeachment, drone strikes,
massive fires in Australia, death of Kobe Bryant,
sex predators' trials. Probably not the start of an
auspicious new year and decade? Surprises daily

As Democrats tussle in Iowa and prepare for
elections, the media blitz is intense. Democracy
appears in arrears and in shambles. Nations spat.
I cocoon inside from the world–just let it rain.

Almost February

Birds are sparse. Even blood-drop,
holly berries seem little compensation
for getting drenched, enduring the cold.

The country wears a gray shroud.
Creatures who hibernate are lucky.
What we witness brings anger, despair.

It has been a wet, gray, foreboding month
with dark events compounding daily.
Today no witnesses for impeachment.

Perhaps next month will be more
upbeat and drier? We are due for
more light to start the new decade?

Senate represents 17% of the nation.
75% of the people wanted witnesses
called. Electoral college is an unjust relic.

We have a president elected not
by popular vote. This list is growing.
Democracy needs a revision.

Much of the nation is depressed.
How different the world could be
if Gore and Clinton took office.

The flu and air pollution make us sick.
Plastic waste insidiously infects us all.
Fires and floods threaten many lives.

The few glints of sun and rare rainbows
encourage us to hold on to hope.
I'm losing my grip and breaking my heart.

Fascinating Discoveries

Birds' eggs in Borneo lead
to ancient cave art of hands
from 40,000 years ago.

Fast radio blasts from space
rarely have a pattern let alone
know what is making FRB'S.

Easter Islanders built moai up
until around 1774. Disease, slavery,
and other impacts lead to culture collapse.

Arroroth, space rock might tell us
how planets are formed. Technology
increases our space discoveries.

Antarctica's Pine Island Glacier known
as PIG has spawned piglets. 115 square
miles being broken into pieces.

Debates about how civilizations
built stone monuments without
tools our times can't reproduce.

The list goes on and on with
so much new data available.
Now discover methods to save us?

Concentrating on Light

When existence seems dark,
seek the light in art, dance, insights
from discoverers in many fields.

When documentaries show
the beauty, skills people
are capable of, I smile gratitude.

My mini-museum exudes color,
texture, mini-creatures, multi-media
arts and crafts. My inner light gets shined.

Finding ways to brighten life
with observations and actions
can give our being a purpose.

I am surrounded by much darkness.
My vision is blurry with cataracts.
Sometimes I cocoon to enlight.

Resilience, determination, tenacity
and hope for a sustainable better world
are needed in these challenging times.

Crack open the light when we can.
With so many well-intentioned people
all living beings and inanimates could thrive.

When Dreaming

Asleep,
we slip between
dimensions, other worlds,
realities, holograms
unknown?

How do
images come?
Cosmic movies, brain blasts,
creative projections on
mind screen?

How do
we control the
content? Take what comes or
depends on type; therapeutic,
vivid?

So far
I request
no nightmares before sleep
has its way with me. I hope for
the best.

What Can We Rely On?

Only
constant is change?
Hard to get a grip when
things keep changing. Rely on hope, faith,
belief?

Might not
hold or protect
you, help you cope or stay.
Nothing to rely on seems is
risky.

Perhaps
change is what we
are to create and learn?
Not even love always sustains us,
can fade.

Only
self-reliance left?
Even that is iffy and
unreliable. Where can we
turn toward?

Maybe
we can't rely
on anything. Just see
what happens? Any control over
our lives?

Casting Shade

In
my
office
shades closed,
I cast shade on our
troubled planet, humanity.

I
can
escape
the TV,
select which screens
to screen out what haunts me daily.

But
I
can not
escape my
feeling sad at world,
despair at unfolding events.

I
cast
shade where
light won't shine,
penetrate the darkness
which pollutes us, wastes our lives.

How
can
I raise
my shades, bring
light? Move from shadows?
Can I disperse some hope? Some love?

This for That

Only in the silence the word, only in dark the light, only in dying life: bright the hawk's flight on the empty sky. Ursula K. Le Guin

Only in the silence, the word.
Only in dark, the light.
Only in dying, life. Bright
the hawk's flight on the empty sky.
　　　You get this from that?
　　　Is this where it's at?

Only in the silence, the word
spoken with various understandings.
We often muddle what is heard.
Words into books by ink brandings.
　　　Imagine if we were hurled
　　　into a silent world.

Only in dark, the light —
a vast multiverse dotted with stars.
Our sun and moon warm our plight.
Are we light-bringing avatars?
　　　Imagine if we were whirled
　　　into a totally dark world.

Only in dying, life. Bright
expectations when born.
Striving to do what's right,
dying feeling sad and forlorn.
　　　Imagine if we gave birth, but did not die.
　　　Would we give this overcrowded world a try?

The hawk's flight on an empty sky
reminds us we're not the only life here.
We see things have gone awry.
Can't wait for a hoped for savior to appear.
　　　We have to deal with earthly conditions.
　　　Bring forth some better renditions?

You get this from that
in this cosmic realm.
Is this where it's at?
Humans tend to overwhelm.
　　　Do we have a choice where we incarnate?
　　　Can we decide how to participate?

The Flow State

We understand that Flow State is a state of uber connection to the universe.
Sara Wiseman

Sara says we know we're in the flow
when we don't feel separate.
Intellectually we can know
we are connected to All, participate
      in magical expansion, this connection.
      But we are involved in self-protection.

When we feel separate
not feeling awe and wonder,
we tend to deliberate
as we toss out the old and ponder.
      We would like our lives to lighten
      and our future outlook to brighten.

Intellectually we can know
this a possibility in our mind,
but we have old misbeliefs to let go
and new ideas to find.
      We'd love to understand
      ways we can expand.

We are connect to all, participate
better when we can enlighten.
What kind of world can we create?
Why so much energy to frighten?
      Not sure I can flow at this stage,
      raise my frequency at my age.

In magical expansion, this connection
could reverse our planet's future.
If we all do some deep reflection,
we could find ways to love and nurture.
      But who can lead us into Flow State?
      It is wonderful to anticipate.

But we are involved in self-protection,
what we believe is right for us and all.
Are we right? Found best detection
for the best way forward and protocol?
      In this 3D duality
      will we get 5D equality?

Holding the World in Your Hands

That's the challenge isn't it, the dark and dire in one hand and the light and hope
in the other. Kathy Ross

Living in a world of duality,
light and dark vie for our attention.
In our hands to balance, seek equality
and select the best intention?
 Without light we cannot see.
 I cringe at attacks on beauty.

Light and dark vie for our attention.
Like a moth I'm drawn to light.
The dark I hesitate to mention,
the source of humanity's plight.
 We seem in the hands of dark leaders.
 Is it light-bringer's job to be weeders?

In our hands to balance, seek equality?
Bring to light issues causing such pain?
Make it clear for all to see?
Try to prevent it from happening again?
 Are we in a resurgence of darkness now?
 Can we spark the light-workers somehow?

And the best intention?
Who will decide and make the changes?
What old beliefs deserve retention?
Can we sustain our planet as climate rearranges?
 I hope my handful of dark and dire
 will open like hands to hope and inspire.

Without light we cannot see.
Are many blind to what we face?
Do they not see the necessity
to revamp the commonplace?
 So many divisions blocking progress,
 miscommunication and greediness.

I cringe at attacks on beauty
and the planetary destruction.
What is my mission's duty?
How long do I wait for instruction?
 Extend a welcoming, helpful hand?
 How long until we understand, take command?

61

Priorities

How do we choose our priorities,
with incomplete, inaccurate information,
considering minorities and majorities,
intentions and situations?
          Look beyond ourselves, serve All?
          How to we find the best protocol?

With incomplete, inaccurate information
we could make deleterious decisions,
join the wrong reformation,
feed greed and divisions.
          Follow our gut
          amid info glut?

Considering minorities and majorities,
how do we make the best choices.
Selfish self-interests, protect seniorities,
listen to a diversity of voices?
          Hear only those who shout the loudest?
          What actions are we the proudest?

Intentions and situations
taken into account?
Viewpoints of differing persuasions
bring tensions, fears mount.
          Is humanity a failed experiment
          or are there new discoveries we can implement?

Look beyond ourselves to serve All?
Do we have the will or the resources?
Are our attempts conditional
on understanding our sources?
          Are we to become "woke" more aware?
          What kind of future will be there?

How do we find the best protocol?
We must play our part, take responsibility?
Is our ignorance and consciousness perpetual?
Do we ever perform to our best ability?
          I can only raise questions,
          not offer cogent suggestions.

Vision Clearing

As my
cataract heals
my vision clears, but what
about insight? Seeing outward?
Inward?

Will my
clarity of
consciousness clear along
with seeing, understanding life
better?

Blurry
borders remain
in divisive, violent
world, polarized, traumatized by
extremes.

Will my
vision ever
truly heal from assaults
on my senses, my hopes and dreams,
always?

So Much to Do

So
much
to do.
Where to start?
What are our choices?
Just what are our priorities?

With
so
many
people, we
face divisions and
power struggles, inequities.

So
much
to do.
Chaotic
world needs our actions
for a sustainable planet.

So
much
to do.
Challenges
to each of us to
do our part, working together.

Who
will
lead us?
Green leaders?
What goals can we reach?
Some global guidelines to adopt?

Climate in Crisis

Seabirds
ill in oceans,
fish plasticized and
Africa has locust plagues
again.

Species
disappear and
diminishing toward their
extinction and we just watch them—
then us?

Air, land
and water are
polluted and weather
changes cause flooding, and more drought
extremes.

Is it
too late to turn
patterns around or are
we victims of our greed, neglect
and waste?

Global To-Do List

The Impeachment trial is underway.
He's at Davos where economists delay.
Greta's there to have her say.

In China a horrible viral flu.
Masked people avoid crowds, achoo.
Several deaths before it's through.

In Australia fire fighters fight.
Blazes leave long-lasting blight.
A very tragic, destructive plight.

In the Middle East tensions brew.
Leaders don't know what to do.
to avoid war over latest hullabaloo.

Plasticized oceans, creatures, polluted air,
earthquakes, droughts everywhere.
climate change deniers, unaware.

People addicted to drugs, screens, cell phone,
vaping, alcohol, homeless, depression prone.
Death by despair suicides feel all alone.

Racism, sexism, wealth inequity divides.
Opinions urge people to take sides.
Quality of life, opportunity slides.

The list goes on–stress unending.
Our future a few are over-spending.
The rest of us are left pending.

I'd love to bury my head in the sand.
So much I wish I could mend and understand.
I can hope light over darkness takes command.

Dances with Books

Cartoons by Grant Snider of book dances with: begin, dive in, page turn, plot twist, melt, leap forward, flip backwards, stretch, bookworm, curl up, release, book drop, bow.

Dancing with books either with body or mind,
increases knowledge, curiosity, imagination.
Book dances spark solos, partnering. I find
even ensembles when choreographed, a vacation
      into experiencing facets explored from the page,
      onto stages, screens, with words we engage.

Increases knowledge, curiosity, imagination
translated into dancing feet.
Dancing in chairs, whatever the motivation
dancing words enhance any feat.
      Whether logical or metaphysical,
      word-dancing makes me quizzical.

Book dances spark solos, partnering I find
with our consciousness as an individual in All.
Keep up the beat. Don't get behind.
Get up, free dance after a fall.
      I seek to become a skilled word-terpsichore
      even when my knees won't let me limb-dance any more.

Even ensembles when choreographed, a vacation—
a chance to be a participant, join in, be free.
Word-dancing is my chosen vocation,
a way to express my creativity.
      When reading a book, your mind dances.
      All the media and ways our life enhances.

Into experiencing facts explored from a page
transfers to screens for more ways to access.
Writing and reading from an early age,
all my life I'm making word-dancing progress.
      Holding a book with eyes word-dancing
      stirs reflection, detection—so life-enhancing

Onto stages, screens with words we engage.
Global communication is available.
Share emotions of love or rage.
Our curiosity is unassailable.
      Book-dancing leads to diverse expression.
      I relish any opportunity for a dancing session.

Express Yourself

When I teach, I seek to open options
for students to express their unique
perspective in their own way.

When I write, I ask questions for
readers to explore and come to their own
conclusions, remain open to new discoveries.

When I think, I venture into new realms
to find new possibilities to enhance
the earthly experiences of all, not just me.

When I choose, I need to weigh possible
impacts. Have I judged fairly? What outmoded
beliefs need to be tossed to make way for new ones?

When I survey the oppression people face,
especially women, I want to protest. If we
do have free will–use it and express yourself!

Writing An American

My friend
introduced me
to American form.
7-6-7 syllables.
Add bug.

Like a
haiku but bugged.
Bug-a-boo to write and
keep tight count, all for focusing
on bug?

No rhyme.
Keep terse and sparse.
I like cinquain better.
Gives me more room to expand on
subjects.

Politics bugs me a lot.
Does most life bug you too?
Are your electronics bugged?

Interrobangs

Behold intense interrobangs,
part question and exclamation,
perfect for heart-felt harangues,
expressing joy and frustration.
When I want to vent and shout,
interrobangs are what it's about.

Part question and exclamation,
a blend of question and exclamation mark,
to forcefully present information,
hit it out of the ballpark.
It's hard to find on my computer,
so I rarely use this transmuter.

Perfect for heart-felt harangues
against injustice and personal hurts.
Use for when your consciousness clangs
and when ideas burst and your best spurts.
I wish I could mark my pages with them.
I could interject them into an anthem.

Expressing joy and frustration,
extremes of emotion come into play.
How can I enhance the situation
and clear a positive pathway?
The energy an interrobang brings,
could be used for better things.

When I want to vent and shout,
make the world pay attention,
I set moral compass to find out
what would be my best intention.
Interrobangs want to display,
what your feelings want to say.

Interrobangs are what it's about,
in this 3D world with light-dark duality.
Interrobangs are two-in-one with clout,
to share your conception of reality.
I have the symbol in blue over my desk.
It's colorful, motivational, picturesque.

Breaking Ranks

At eighty I will break ranks
with old ideas,
say no thanks.

All the isms that divide us
I'll take a stand or
put aside.

We must sustain a future
no deniers, we're
to nurture.

Not all about "me".
Wake up! See!

Emotional Climate

Society as a whole benefits immeasurably
from a climate in which all persons,
regardless of race or gender, may have
an opportunity to earn respect,
responsibility, advancement and
remuneration based on ability.

Sandra Day O'Conner

Creating Reality

As grime and glitter splays before us,
reality covered up under layers of denial,
I'm tired of preaching to a chorus.
I'm weary of judging, putting things on trial.
> Some days are leaden, damp and gray.
> I do not like living this way.

Reality covered up under layers of denial,
a sense of futility encroaches our souls.
What can we contribute that is worthwhile?
How do we perform our desired roles?
> Through words we speak, the costumes we wear–
> how can we become "woke" and aware?

I'm tired of preaching to a chorus
my perceived panic and urgency.
So many people just ignore us.
They do not see an emergency.
> Maybe I'm over-reacting.
> My point of view too exacting?

I'm weary of judging, putting things on trial,
examining for truth, doubting sources.
I get exhausted and meanwhile
the planet runs out of resources.
> Are we coming to the realization
> we are nearing the end of this civilization?

Some days are leaden, damp and gray.
Conditions weigh heavily, elicit tears.
Color seems to drain away.
We are left to face our fears.
> When we feel so oppressed,
> it is hard not to become depressed.

I do not like living this way.
I want light, sun, sustainability.
I want all people to have a say
and contribute to their best ability.
> I am becoming an angry screamer.
> I want to uplift, to become a dreamer.

Dark Chocolate Savior

When I'm down, a dark chocolate savior
can save me with bites of a delicious bar.
Dark chocolate sweetens my behavior.
Uplifted I wish upon a star.
       Somehow the world seems less dark.
       Chocolate ignites my spark.

Can save me with bites of a delicious bar
stuffed near my computer in a drawer.
Gently I open the file cabinet ajar
to feel my spirit restored once more.
       What if there is no stash there?
       I must not be negligent and prepare.

Dark chocolate sweetens my behavior.
I plunk keys, release my mind.
I preach and sing with my choir.
Who knows what I will find
       with dark chocolate as a spur?
       What surprises can occur?

Uplifted I wish upon a star,
somehow gird to endure Earth's pangs.
With chocolate not very far,
I sort through various harangues,
       wonder about realities and fantasies
       multidimensional possibilities and mysteries.

Somehow the world seems less dark,
keep dark in chocolate, my antidote
to heaviness, my place to park
my misgivings, explore a new quote.
       Fueled by chocolate my vision expands.
       Deep inside me my soul understands.

Chocolate ignites my spark
though all may be be an illusion.
It creates a place to embark
and might lead to a conclusion.
       The world appears much brighter
       with my dark chocolate ignitor.

Typing with Dark Chocolate

Chocolate bits slip between
the keys and clog them—
messy scene.

Must sit back from the keyboard
to safely enjoy,
my sweet horde.

I pause to chew, peruse screen.
Husband vacuumed keys–
not tech queen.

Mood like chocolate bar,
glows like star.

A Sad Friend

A good friend suffers great pain,
family troubles,
fears again.

She sees problems for loved ones
she can't control or
make undone.

Witnessing such hard anguish
for loved ones, a
healing wish.

She hopes for some peace,
for release.

After the Fall

Recently I fell twice so
called in firemen.
Pride felt blow.

I've no broken bones, but sore–
in body and mind
Want no more.

I try to pay attention.
Accidents happen.
Intention?

Why must I do this?
I'm clueless.

News Vacation

Can take just so much of news
before I need break
from fake clues.

A break from darkness, despair
over world condition—
too aware.

Headlines flutter across page.
Killings, victims, lies.
I feel rage.

Give me light TV.
Best for me.

Unanswerable

Each question has an answer?
Some unknowable?
No chancers?

We're trying to understand
what life is about?
Take command?

We don't ask the right questions?
Truth is misleading?
Suggestions?

Some things I don't know.
Remain so?

Inundated

Overloaded with data
on screen and page.
Stigmata?

Sift and sort what to absorb.
Is all recorded
in cloud orb?

What do I need to know, do?
What will I reject
when I'm through.

When pondering my life–
joy or strife?

Successful Activism

People around the world are angry. They don't have a say in things that matter in their lives. So they protest, sign petitions and organized sit-ins. How can we make them add up to something more so people have power. Hahrie Han

We start the new decade with unsustainable
wealth distribution and environmental degradation.
A viable future seems futile and unattainable.
It is a time to change, bring new organization.
      People power depends not on what they have
      but how they use power and behave.

Wealth distribution and environmental degradation
require leadership to solve our world's problems, not donors.
Six experts studied six organizations for investigation.
How they handle "Metrics for success"— a corporation honors.
      Build skills to hold people in power accountable.
      Put hands on levers of change. Be responsible.

A viable future seems futile and unattainable.
Time for organizations to do some changing.
What acts are sustainable?
What goals need re-arranging?
      Put people in settings where they can build connections,
      negotiate their preferred selections.

It is a time to change, bring new organization.
Leaders need to feel urgency to change status quo.
Too long we fear and live in frustration.
We need people and leaders in position to know
      where to commit energies to solve
      problems of the planet with higher resolve.

People power depends on not what they have
but to form coalitions for the greater good.
We have a planet and future to save.
Time to act collectively as we should.
      Coalitions can increase the pace
      of progress for the human race.

But how they use powfaer and behave
can lead to our renewal or extinction.
Ask what greed took? Ponder what they gave?
Will this anthropocene era have the distinction
      of ending the viability of Earth?
      Or will it witness a rebirth?

Multidimensional Me

When dreaming I am inter-dimensional.
Asleep in the cosmos, awake in 3D.
Wafting in and out of time, multidimensional—
new faces, new places, moving agilely.
 How many dimensions do I experience being
 sentient, conscious, actually seeing?

Asleep in the cosmos, awake in 3D
are more lives outside my awareness?
Am I in more than one reality?
Am I a bio-being, formless, breathing, airless?
 In dreams like imagination there are different rules.
 I'm able to do things beyond earthly 3D duals.

Wafting in and out of time, multidimensional
beings come from memories, conjured
from demands of the environment, intentional
illusions to protect the hale and injured?
 Do our lives fork at every decision?
 We live out each choice and provision?

New faces, new places, moving agilely
through unknown conditions toward what mission?
Do I learn of a new turn, new ability
with each exploration or transmission?
 Can I call anywhere really home
 if eternally I'm fated to roam?

How many dimensions do I experience being
part of some cosmological quest?
Why am I always coping, foreseeing,
wondering at my end as an experimental test?
 Have I discovered a respite in all my travels?
 How many times am I there as a planet unravels?

Sentient, conscious, actually seeing?
Or trapped in an unknown fog of delusion?
I hope for this planet's well-being,
but find myself dealing with confusion.
 Can I be part of light-filled lives
 in a multiverse where all thrives?

Dream Symbols

Last night's dream I comforted
visitors- parents with three children
grieving the loss of an infant.

Two developers building white
towers tried to poison the interiors
of the other's building. People—pawns.

I ride many cars and elevators
in and out of realities–snippets
of what I observe on Earth.

In other realms I know people
and landscapes not available
here and I have greater mobility.

When we dream do we dip into
multidimensional aspects of our soul?
Simultaneous lives ƒat different frequencies?

I don't like nightmares, darkness.
Fortunately they are not common.
But when they appear, I fear.

Depends how we view the cosmic role
in any of our possible lives. Are we to
focus on Earth during this embodiment?

If we are all citizens of the cosmos,
experiencing various forms and places,
what is the purpose? What are we to learn?

Do dreams give hints at what is out there?
Will we chose our next life's manifestation?
If we chose to come here, how best to serve?

Dreams do not always guide us. Fantasies?
Respites? Whatever their purpose, the sleep
is welcome for tired spirits and weary bones.

The Immigrant Waves

I was in an art class with about ten students.
The teacher said we were to enter an art contest.
I am not big on contests, so I suggested
we paint a towering wave crashing on the shore.

Each painter added a layer of green and blue
until we had a surfer's delight of a wave.
It foamed on the shore. The teacher wanted
my name on the entry since it was my idea.

I did not want to do it. I wanted it to be
a group entry–a symbolic wave of immigrants
arriving on U.S. shore. The students were diverse
and the wave was cooperatively magnificent.

I decided to make my own wave with layers of color
to indicate migrations. At the base was a brown tone
for Native Americans, then white for Europeans, black
for Africans, yellow for Asians, a shade of brown for Mexicans.

It was shaped like a wave and I blended the colors
at the edges to show melding. I added more layers
for Central Americans, repeats for other migrations.
The tides spilled on the ground–glistening.

Fuzzy as dreams are, I think one of the waves won
a prize, but not sure which one–or care. Was I musing
the cover for my book Waves? Reflecting at the global
migrations due to climate change? Waves roll on.

Did I Sign Up for This?

Was I drafted before I incarnated?
Did I come from my free will?
My hopes for Earth are devastated.
The planet warms while I chill.
What are we here to do?
Will we achieve a breakthrough?

Did I come from my free will
aware of the challenges of life here?
Am I prepared with adequate skill
to deal with and clear atmosphere?
Many of us are dispirited
by the planet we inherited.

My hopes for Earth are devastated
by inept leadership, misguided missions.
I see darkness unfold as light waited
to shine forth uplifting transmissions.
Where are good ideas to guide us?
Are there any light-beings beside us?

The planet warms as I chill
deep into my bones with fear.
I cling to hope, try to cope until
we manage to clean up the earthly sphere.
Sadly I have concluded,
air, land and sea are polluted.

What are we here to do?
Truly I am not alone who guesses.
Anyone in charge—a committee? Who?
How are we to repair our messes.
Life is becoming less sustainable
on a planet becoming less maintainable.

Will we achieve a breakthrough?
Are we about to run out of solutions and time?
Will we manage to blunder through?
Will we commit a cosmic crime?
Failed to steward planet, resist, persist?
Very hard to remain an optimist.

What's Wrong With That?

That is a nuisance to me and does not
clarify in many cases. Sounds harsh.
That can be dropped with no loss of meaning.

Imagine that? What's the matter with that?
That thing you do... That problem, that time,
that will inspire, that jerk...

That can be a pronoun. That's a good idea.
That can be a determiner. Where is that
child of yours? Look at that man there.

That can be an adverb. I would not go
that far. That can be a conjunction. Oh
that she could be restored to health.

That seems a lazy word. That clutters
more than clears. I try to rewrite lines
in which that appears...except in this rant.

Nine of the top 100 quotes contain that. All but
one— long dead men. #3 was Aristotle: *It is during
our darkest moments that we must focus to see the light.*

Other examples. Mahatma Ghandi. *Be the change
that you wish to see in the world.* Edgar Allan Poe:
All that we see or seem to see is but a dream within a dream.

John Keats: *I love you the more in that I believe
you had liked me for my own sake and nothing else.*
We do not need that in any of these.

A.P. Abdul Kalam: *Let us sacrifice our today
so that our children can have a better tomorrow.*
Swami Vivebananda focuses on that one idea your life.

Thomas Carlyle: *...that in all things distinguishes
the strong soul from the weak.* In his opinion.
Henry James: *Do not mind anything that anyone tells you...*

Then that girl Margaret Mead: *Always remember
that you are absolutely unique. Just like everyone else.*
It's just that I do not like to use that.

Mini-bits of Joy

In my mini-museum on walls,
on surfaces, color and whimsy,
smiling creatures, spots of art calls
for my attention to fantasy.
          Mini-bits of joy brighten.
          Each day they lighten.

On surfaces color and whimsy
shine and glow for all to enjoy.
Their crowded presence theoretically
could bring claustrophobia and annoy.
          But only a few feel that way.
          I invite mini-bits of joy to stay.

Smiling creatures, spots of art calls
my heart and soul to uplift.
Just their presence recalls
glee in collection, someone's gift.
          My mini-museum is extraordinary,
          sets apart my home from the ordinary.

For my attention to fantasy,
creativity, mini-bits spark
light on imagination and ecstasy
to rescue reality from the dark.
          Many are angels, seasonal kinds—
          thousands of joy dots, treasured finds.

Mini-bits of joy brighten
mood, insights bring hope
humanity will enlighten,
be better able to cope.
          We view the world with different filters,
          try to realign when planet off-kilters.

Each day they lighten
whatever burden wears me down.
I smile at them and tighten
my grip, uplift my frown.
          For a little while I like what I see—
          the art from delightful creativity.

Memories from Sweden

Four times I visited the homeland
of my four grandparents. Twice
I went to conferences with my husband
and twice to meet my Swedish relatives.

One time we took our son and three
grandchildren. We rented a van
and had a wonderful time. My mother
and I went before we knew these relatives.

There is always someone to translate
when I garble attempts at Swedish
or someone struggles with English.
There are times I wish my grandparents stayed.

We saw the farm one grandfather left from.
Various family graves and Swedish events,
with family guides made visits memory-packed.
They also had my genealogy back centuries.

Family stories delighted. I learned of a poet
relative–one grandmother's half-brother who
had a very difficult youth and struggles
to self-educate while working farm labor.

But it is the living Swedes I treasure. Such
kind, generous, warm people. Sweden today
is a model for the world. I doubt many Swedes
are leaving at this time. They gave us Greta Thunberg.

I created books about our visits and shared with
all branches. Now my cousin's family has gone
as well. Just today I received an email of the Swedes
celebrating a 92nd birthday–all together.

We keep in touch by emails. Love the photos
of these very photogenic relatives. I am proud
of my Swedish ancestry. Learning about my
relatives has been a blessing in my life.

Euchred

Australian Informal. Yoo-kerd. Utterly done in or at the end of one's tether; exhausted. Dictionary,com

Australians must be euchred with record-breaking fire.
Americans are euchred with Donald Trump.
The global situation with climate change is dire.
The ocean's garbage patches a plastic dump.
       I am definitely feeling euchred, obscured.
       World-wide fake news and lies heard.

Americans are euchred with Donald Trump
narrowly escaping starting WW3.
He spews nonsense, followers jump,
destroys Constitution and democracy.
       With Senate and Supreme Court stacked,
       the impeachment biased, integrity lacked.

The global situation with climate change is dire.
Extreme weather, hurricanes, flooding, burning.
Many leaders take the stance of denier.
Where are the solutions we are learning?
       Many react with marches, petitions, outrage.
       Time's running out, we must each engage.

The oceans garbage patches a plastic dump.
Plastic crumbles into micro-pellets on the shore.
Soon more plastic in seas than fish to pump
more plastic into every being than ever before.
       Glaciers calve, pollution and sea levels rise.
       Forests and species decline Any compromise?

I am definitely feeling euchred, obscured.
Our women's Huddle is traumatized
by the fake and real news deterred—
insanity. We are less and less surprised.
       Despite some upbeat prophesies,
       the Earth is shrouded in atrocities.

World-wide fake news and lies heard.
Greedy wealthy exploit the poor.
What is the power in science, art, one's word?
Have we run out of options to explore?
       Inequity, division, Old World hierarchies spark
       New World ideas to enlighten the dark?

Rainy Day Haircut

My windblown hair, rain-speckled jacket,
blew into the hair salon. When I checked in
there was a 35 minutes wait. A man after me
walked right back out into the storm.

I read a Southwest Art magazine and only waited
15 minutes for a young man with tattooed arms,
baseball cap, dressed in black to call my name.

I had not been to the salon in four months,
he had worked there for three. I do not usually
have my hair-washed, but I'd had a very busy day.

He must have winced when he saw a disheveled
white-haired, old lady dressed in blue and a navy hoodie push
a walker to his station. He was a gentle, pleasant man,

the age of my eldest grandson, who had a father my age.
We had both given up dying our hair and liked
the same colors. He had worked in a tattoo parlor.

He designed the tattoos as a graphic designer.
He was meticulous cutting my bushy hair, like
a sculptor slowly adding details.

Going into the haircut, perhaps we both had
stereotypical expectations. I had trouble sitting
in the chairs because of the foot bar.

I walked to the washing basin without the walker.
He assured me his support and shoulder to lean on
if needed. As we chatted I learned more and more.

He massaged my head. The massage I had before
coming there did not massage my head–she
warm-stoned and oiled my agitated and sore body.

Before my massage and haircut I was alarmed
about the well-being of a friend–very stressed. Fortunately
I had some downtime before the haircut.

We talked easily. My hair and first impressions
clipped. As I walked out into the rainy afternoon,
I felt lighter. I tussled with my walker, then drove home.

It had been a stressful week of Trump
starting, then applauded himself for
not igniting World War 3.

In the hair salon my hope for a peaceful
world, based on cooperation and not
relying on first impression was renewed.

Maybe I should not wait so long between
haircuts. My bangs were hanging too low.
I bought some fast food with slow service,

as I drove home. By 3:30 I was taking a nap—
solid sleep not like night before. When I woke,
it was dark. I turned on the light inside and out.

Deciding Criteria

How
to
decide
what to do?
Just experiment?
Creative choice? Fad or science?

How
to
create
my dreams, goals?
Curiosity?
Playful discovery? Set plan?

How
to
choose plans
wisely or
from several — guess?
Fantasy, whimsy, or blindly?

I
spend
too much
time thinking.
Act on impulse and
regret it? Try alternatives?

I
might
not get
the best pick.
Criteria not
clear? Sometimes just have to wing it?

Your Life's Calling

*Can you state your life's calling in one sentence?... When you know what you
are here to do, it makes it much easier to do it.* Sara Wiseman

Some people take many years or decades,
to understand what they are to contribute to the whole.
We all must face some upgrades.
Some geniuses innately know their role.
> Hints and nudges from the universe
> suggest what you might rehearse?

To understand what they are to contribute to the whole
helps them experience what they are meant to do.
Some bypass a lot of rigamarole
and make a quicker breakthrough.
> We are here to learn our contribution?
> Whose in charge of distribution?

We all must face some upgrades
as our awareness and consciousness expands.
We try to avoid retrogrades
when we take our destiny into our own hands.
> Is our calling coded before we're born?
> We'll discover some oath we have sworn?

Some geniuses innately know what to do.
Child prodigies or result of an accident,
they are highly creative, while the rest have no clue?
They set a high bar and a new precedent.
> The rest of us muddle along the way
> until a higher being becomes our mainstay?

Hints and nudges from the universe
should be listened to and respected.
We need to connect and converse.
No one should be neglected.
> But lives for many of us are appalling.
> They await knowledge of their calling.

Suggest what you might rehearse
and act upon should your calling becomes clear?
What conditions can you reverse?
Can you uplift Earth's atmosphere?
> I hope cosmic beings align
> and help humans beat a deadline.

Dancing Despair Away

Dance is an antidote to despair; in this hard and divided world, when we dance together, we express ourselves creatively as one. Sandra J. Bean

From the many suggestions
how to deal with despair
over our insidious situations,
the best one I am aware–
> dance for some temporary relief.
> Dance would uplift my belief.

How to deal with despair
has several approaches,
with so many areas to repair
we might need several coaches.
> Counseling and pills could be expensive.
> The treatments could be intensive.

Over our insidious situations
looms a doom's day futility.
We need inclusive conversations
of some effectiveness and utility.
> Many are overwhelmed and weary
> having tried theory after theory.

The best one I am aware
that would perk me up is dance.
But less mobile I would not dare
to return to dance which would enhance
> my joy and feeling free.
> But now dance can't be done by me.

Dance for some temporary relief
for ritual, creative expression.
No matter the pattern or motif,
on stage or in a community session,
> dance can express unity, joining hands
> by-pass differences, focus on dance demands.

Dance could uplift my belief
as no religion or organization can.
Even if my dance time was brief
I am a devoted dance fan.
> Dance to create joy and beauty—
> out of love not sense of duty.

Jo

Jo– beloved one, darling, sweetheart. Dictionary.com

Jo's another word for a loved one,
part of a name like Jo March or Jolene
Some named Jo we might shun
prefer maybe pet, or friend, not libertine.
> More words for love are welcome.
> We all want to find some.

Part of a name like Jo March or Jolene ,
Jo Jo Rabbit, Joe Jonas, My Pal Joey?
Mary's husband, Joe Kennedy- keen
on Joe Biden or ones more showy?
> A wide range of Jo choices-
> Jose, Joanne hear our voices?

Some named Jo we might shun
like Joe Stalin– one of the worst.
There are other Jo's for everyone.
Not all Jo's are cursed.
> So pick a Jo that shares your love.
> Anyone you are especially thinking of?

Prefer maybe a pet, friend, not libertine
but one who supports you in kindly ways,
brings joy and laughter, doesn't demean.
Some Jo beaus are brief and some will stay.
> Jo's melt our hearts
> like the words on Sweet Tarts.

More words to love are welcome.
Finding Jo's can cause some frustration.
When one is found, one can become
happy in one's newly found situation.
> Some folks have many Jo's
> bringing joy and sometimes woes.

We all want to find some
love, compassion, good intentions.
Wherever our chosen ones come from,
we hope they are positive interventions.
> Hope our joeys are not like a kangaroo
> who soon hops away and leaves you.

The Numerology of Love
It turns out the numerology of love is 21 or 3. Melanie Beckler

Apparently 21 is the number symbolic of success
and the fulfillment of desire. Is this just for Eros
and not other kinds of love? Depends on how defined?

3 is a number for individuality, creativity,
charisma and cheerfulness. Helpful
for sustaining a relationship?

Love is a feeling not a number. Words
do not always express love well, actions
might be more clear if positive.

Apparently numbers vibrate and can
raise your vibration. Open up to your
real self and truth. Still numbers seem edgy.

She suggests to simply breathe light into
your heart and let your heart light open
and expand to illuminate the highest possibilities.

When dealing with the many kinds of love,
we try different approaches. How do you
quantify success in love?

Choose Love

Love is not complicated but it's complex. We all long for love, are made of love, thrive on love and will risk much to give and receive it. Melanie Beckler

As Valentine's Day approaches our thoughts
turn to love and our experiences with it.
Memories, losses, current status–Greeks
described seven kinds of love. Pick and choose.

Eros- Love of the body. Sexual attraction for
others. Modern romantic love. Often fades fast.
Lose control, poor judgment. Root in sacral chakra.
Pinnacle and pit of desire. Highly emotional.

Philia- Affectional love of friends and family.
Companionship, friendship, trust and values
mutually shared and reciprocated. Heart chakra.
Can become intense and experience glitches.

Storge- love of a child. Child received acceptance,
forgiveness, comfort, nurturing, security, safety,
sacrifice. Born of dependency. Bond can become
frayed and cut. Heart chakra really challenged.

Agape- Selfless, universal love for all humanity,
Mother Earth and the Divine. Angels say keep
choosing love in every moment. Charity, unselfish
concern, highest interest of all connects to 7 chakras.

Ludus- Playful love. Seduction, flirtation, sex
experience without attachment. Teasing, euphoria,
Keep love fresh. Not predators. Must be mutual
or it is abusive. Tread carefully before playing.

Pragma- Couples together for many years, moved
beyond physical. Easy harmony and balance. They
maintain and nurture love. Compromise, patience,
tolerance. Standing not falling in love. Root and heart chakras.

Philautia- Love of self. Sense of belonging and
purpose. Self-love and worth. Not hubris or narcissism.
Not fame, wealth, pleasure. Healthy and unhealthy ways.
Love self to truly love others. Heart and 3rd eye chakras.

Many kinds of valentines to give–positive and negative.
More love is welcome everywhere by everyone.

Feeling Grumpy

Feeling grumpy,
down in the dumpy
because of Humpty-Trumpty.

Feeling grumpy lately
because my body's sore and achy.
World's deteriorating greatly.

Feeling grumpy because
darkness will not pause
and much of the cause.

Feeling grumpy, in the dark.
Looking for a light spark,
seeking a place to a disembark.

Feeling grumpy hurts.
Joy comes in spurts.
Painful alerts.

Feeling grumpy is a bummer.
March to a different drummer?
Become a hummer or a mummer?

True to Form

When I
write, I try free
verse, but return to forms.
Forms line up my scattered thoughts, to
corral.

As my
ideas flow
I seek pattern, order,
a way to enhance clarity,
inform.

Sometimes
the feelings are
intense and seek escape.
Forms shape them, contain, create new
poems.

At times
I go with flow,
free to scramble down lines,
set loose these restraints, break rules to
create.

I like
syllable counts,
rhyme schemes and set patterns
to word-play and resolve each word
puzzle.

Poems
are terse. Unlike
prose which has own tricks. I
prefer to be true to poems
and forms.

From the Other Side Honey Joins Us for Scrabble

When I play Cooperative Scrabble,
my mother, everyone called Honey,
comes to join us, earthly rabble.
Creating her name makes me sunny.
        Sometimes up to five times,
        my unearthly mother chimes.

My mother, everyone called Honey
was a creative teacher and artist.
She never created art for money.
She was a homebound perfectionist.
        Her home was her creative outlet.
        It's charm I will never forget.

Comes to join us–earthly rabble
every game and makes her presence known.
We discard the rules and babble
about her and the world, have grown
        accustomed to thinking of her,
        as she makes her cosmic transfer.

Creating her name makes me sunny.
She loved strawberries and sunflowers,
green, yellow, holiday decorations. Funny
how I collect miniatures too, as her love-showers
        shoot rays of light,
        memories of delight.

Sometimes up to five times
my mother's name appears.
Letter by letter my anticipation climbs.
When game over, she's part of our cheers.
        I relax after the first of Honey horde
        plops her arrival on the board.

My unearthly mother chimes
into my thoughts and memories.
Messages from the sublime
penetrate my reveries.
        To feel she is still here to play,
        somehow lightens my earthbound stay.

Facing Eye Surgeries

Two dates are set to remove cataracts.
I'm blurry, leery, rely on hope.
My mind struggles with the facts.
I need to gear up courage to cope.
       It's scary to fear loss of eyesight.
       Vision is the source of my insight.

I'm blurry, leery, rely on hope.
I plop three drops four times a day.
I want to clarity my scope,
to witness clearly on my way.
       I am uncomfortable with the thought
       that probably surgery will be for naught.

My mind struggles with the facts.
I'll need a pillow at head and knees
to help me breathe and prop knees- acts
required for me to feel comfortable, more at ease.
       I envision something might go wrong.
       and my poor vision might prolong.

I need to gear up courage to cope
with my anxiety and fears.
Can I reverse this slippery slope?
My eyes have been "unripe" for years.
       Now they attempt to make me clear-eyed,
       I ponder why it took so long to decide.

Its scary to fear loss of eyesight.
I can't type without looking at keys.
Most cases the surgery comes out all right,
it's quick and easy, a breeze.
       What if I sneeze, want to cough.
       Will they call the surgery off?

Vision is the source of my insight
I can't rely sorely on my mind.
Much of the basis of what I write,
depends on what I learn and find.
       I am feeling very stressed.
       Will my surgeries be blessed?

Is My Life Worth Coming For?

Apparently I incarnated reluctantly,
encouraged to answer Earth's call
for volunteers to help with Earth's plight.
Uplift Earth's protocol?

I do not know if this is true
or how predestined is our birth.
Unclear what I am supposed to do,
and what my attempts are worth.

Apparently we have angelic guardians,
perhaps a DNA code inserted?
I don't like unknowable limbo.
At times I feel deserted.

I like the concept of angels.
I collect miniature replicas.
I guess they ignite hope and light
for world–not just America's.

I'll never know why I came.
Just part of unanswered questions.
Alone within All to muddle through.
Can't rely on cosmic suggestions.

Backward Hoodies

Today
my husband and
I both put our hoodies
on backwards. Faces masked, blocked and
darkened.

He does
this often, but this
is rare for me. Pants and
socks get me stuck more often, like
daily.

I took
it as a bad
omen and start for day.
I struggled to turn it around,
free face.

Shoulder
sore and annoyed
I looked for glitches to
come, being more vigilant and
cautious.

I pulled
hoodie over
eyes for a nap to keep
warming sunshine on my bed and
to sleep.

Typing,
my hoodie's down
cuddling my neck, nestling.
Will I wear hoodie tomorrow?
Maybe.

Cocooning

As I
rest from left eye
cataract surgery.
I type one-eyed with black patch like
pirate.

I nap
more, use screens less.
Quiet anxiety with
deep breathing, uplifting thoughts to
coccoon.

Outside
sirens, traffic.
Inside try to be still,
tranquil, diminished energy
to heal.

I need
to mellow about
a week longer, then the
right eye a month later, to heal
again.

Blurry
sight, like typing
through tears the world evokes.
Clear-eyed vision needed to solve world's
problems.

Viral Greetings: No Touchy-Feelies

Handshakes
and hugs are not
welcome viral season.
Masks and gloves maintain boundaries,
and health.

Greeters
develop routines–
knee to knee, and elbow to
elbow. Wave arms, stomp feet, bow head,
invent.

Greeters
in flu season
are aware of close contact.
Crowds are germy, encouraged to
stay home.

Wash hands.
Do not touch face.
Regular advice on
overdrive. Talk on internet
or phone.

Correct
information
hard to find, as people
hoard food and meds, quarantine in
their home.

But air
pollution down.
Jobs on layoff, global
economy effected as we
greet less.

Good time
to hibernate,
cocoon indoors, read book.
greet world electronically,
relax?

Boosters

Echinacea, Goldenseal, Osha root, Elberberry,
Oregano, Astragalus–an immune system booster.
With pills and oils, meds and vitamins, we can
become pill popper, self-medicator, eager juicer,

We can also boost spirits with other rituals,
belief systems or morale uplifter.
Distractions, inactions, creative blocks—
times as absent-minded drifters.

Energy drinks, dark chocolate, sugar
make my enjoyment and energy rise.
I seek a boost with positivity, light.
At eighty I'm less energetic I surmise.

I appreciate all kinds of boost.
Makes me feel I claim my roost.

Returning Refrigerator Magnets

After a recent cleaning of the fridge front,
all the magnets were put in a box–stored.
The white-faced door looked pale, colorless.

Usually amid the angels, animals, tourist sites
and event magnets are newspaper clippings, comic
strips, photos, poem posters, postcards, Obama.

Entombed for months, I missed their spots
of color and word-play. Now that I am sheltering
in place, I have time, no excuse not to rescue them.

I created a folder for the excess, to reduce clutter.
I will exchange them for those in the spotlight
when we either wash the door or I change places.

One by one I found a spot for the magnets,
they may hold different articles. Some hold
medical information for easy access.

I filled the barren plane, remembering where
I bought them, if they were gifts. Some origins
fade from memory. I appreciate designs and color.

I live in a mini-museum filed with thousands
of seasonal and perennial creatures. Angels
roost everywhere. I had neglected these magnets.

In this time of isolation these light spots console.
Now a few more on the refrigerator–more the merrier.
A black jointed, lanky body can move positions.

This gender-less, hairless flat form changes postures
according to the whim of a passerby. I position the
limbs as a graceful dancer ready to dance.

Control

If I'm
given control,
over what would I want?
I don't have full control over
myself.

Power
can corrupt. I
might not maintain my best
intentions under confusion,
duress.

What Earth
rules could I change?
Cosmos seems to hold strings.
DNA coding rigid? Any free
will left?

Many
unanswered "why's".
How can I lead if I
am not sure of my choices, for what
intent?

Those in
control tend to
cause inequality,
division, injustice, increase
their greed.

For what
would I seek this
control? Restore justice?
How far would my reach be? Can I
help all?

I don't
need the spotlight,
just free to create and
grow mentally, not weight-wise, as
I write.

Events
spin out of our
control. Go with the flow?
What force is in control of the
cosmos?

Dark/light
duality
seems essence of our Earth's
reality. Shine the light? We'll
want to?

Control
to me is just
a theoretical
conundrum. Turn effort to what
can change?

I'll try
some strategies
to help me cope and hope,
know I've little control over
outcome.

Whirligig

Sometimes
I feel like a
whirligig, changing and
whirling in a spiraling world-
spinning.

So much
to intake and
process, sort out for my
priorities to contemplate for
action.

Input
may not be that
reliable and outcomes
murky as intentions are
hidden.

Even
if understood
and decision is clear,
I may not want to support them.
Bad vibes.

How are
we to sift for
the best result with
sustainable and inclusive
info?

People
place barriers
to others' rights to choose
what is their best without hurting
others.

With so
many people
holding opposite views,
just how do we choose what is best
for all?

In Chaotic and Stressful Times

It's normal to have anxious thoughts–yet you can calm them down. It's normal to worry in times of stress–yet there are ways to worry less. Sara Wiseman

You can use four discernments for anxious thought:
Is it real? Is it here? Is it now? Is it mine?
Double down on your spiritual practice ought
to help. Recommit to your self care, find
      ways to remember you are an infinite soul.
      Can you try to improve your earthly role?

Is it real? Is it here? Is it now? Is it mine?
Probing for answers is not an easy task.
Answers could be a personal gold mine.
For guidance who can we ask?
      Divinations? Gurus, Angels, Professionals?
      Read? Attend lectures and confessionals?

Double down on your spiritual practice ought
to assist. Meditate, pray, give worries to angels?
Connect to your guides, but if for naught
try to approach by other angles.
      Not everyone has a spiritual practice to use.
      What about those who would refuse?

To help, re-commit to your self-care, find
more nature, more sleep, more exercise.
Deep breathe, eat healthy, find peace of mind
watching comedies, talk to friends, be wise.
      Whatever makes you feel safe and whole.
      Deal with your own rigamarole.

Ways to remember you are an infinite soul
who explores and expands through many lives.
This is just your current earthly gig, roll
with the flow and whatever good thrives.
      Lifetime after lifetime we experience to learn.
      When is a life-break, vacation I earn?

Can you try to improve your earthly role?
What's the flip side to worry and stress.
Find some methods to cajole.
Enjoy some joy and happiness.
      Do we all discover ways to deal
      with what is illusion or real and heal?

Tolerance for Ambiguity

Once I adopted tolerance for ambiguity
as my New Year's resolution. Now I find
I am not that tolerant of ambiguity.

Being capable of being understood
in more than one way is not the clarity
I seek from the murkiness of unreliable inputs.

I want more unity, progress on climate
and social problems, peace, cooperation,
compassion, our best intentions.

I did not make a New Year's resolution
even though it is not just a new year,
but a new decade. My hopes are unclear.

Abstract ideas seek concrete expression.
I do prefer letters to numbers, a more
liberal slant. Creativity and curiosity are goals.

I'll just be a light-seeker, temporarily
assigned to Earth by some cosmic plan,
trying to make the best of physical 3D duality.

If I am multidimensional and my soul is
eternally expanding consciousness
beyond time and all over the cosmos–

who knows how long I have been dealing
with ambiguity. Wonder if I was ever truly
tolerant? Wonder how this lifetime compares?

Social Climate

Go to Heaven for the climate,
Hell for the company.
Mark Twain

Making New Year's Resolutions

With over half abandoning their resolutions
by February, any takers for a decade?
Adding radical changes, any revolutions?
In what areas are you seeking an upgrade?
What concepts will be put on trial?
In what areas do you remain in denial?

By February, (any takers for a decade?)
our best intentions likely fall by the wayside.
What new ideas try to persuade
you toward unity, not toward divide?
Are you thinking of the long run?
Just basking in the shade from the sun?

Adding radical changes, any revolutions
lure you toward urgent actions?
Are you pondering new solutions?
Finding new interactions?
How prone to risk? How committed?
Your lack of enlightenment admitted?

In what areas are you seeking an upgrade?
How inward or outward? How far your outreach?
Do you accept a global retrograde?
Face obstacles you are unable to breach?
Is your will not up to match your heart?
How much do you want to take part?

What concepts will be put on trial?
What beliefs require examination?
Louder or downward turn of the dial?
What will be your final determination?
One day at a time? Longer outlook?
Have you reflected on the path you took?

In what areas do you remain in denial?
What is reality and what is illusion?
What delusional thoughts to throw on junk pile?
Are you able to come to any conclusion?
As new decade starts I hope to remain open,
be involved and explore what will happen.

114

Adorning Identity

"Why are you wearing a safety pin on your shirt?"
I answered, "It means you are safe with me."
The safety pin means I would stand up to bullies,
sexists and racists, bonk them with my walker,
to protect someone vulnerable or report them.

I have an orange bow ribbon on my knit hat
from some march, but I forget which cause.
I have a blue ribbon and an angel on a coat.
I have worn yellow and red bows as well. I'd like
a green bow to support environmentalists.

But what about hair color and tattoos?
Certain groups have clear opinions.
Some religions decide which sex is more
empowered and discriminate against
those who love and marry those they oppose.

Skin color and gender bring expectations
which can be totally erroneous. You have
no control over the skin color you wear.
Choices of clothes and hair styles evoke
prejudices. We seem easy to judge.

Buttons, head gear, uniforms proclaim affiliations
say something about interests and allegiances.
I have a collection of buttons which polka dot
a cardboard file box. Blobs of color I enjoy.
Personalities express in diverse ways.

Today an acquaintance identified as white,
American, Christian. I resist labeling. I guess
if pressed—Earthling, cosmic citizen and poet who
collects angels and adorns herself in a lot of blue.
I am wary of "isms", but of feminist, liberal ilk.

The presence we present to the world as
an individual and member of a group can
matter. There are many divisions with haters
and deniers causing violence and chaos.
Should we more aware of what we project?

Word of the Decade

Singular pronoun "they" is named word
of the decade by language experts — depends,
if linguists pay attention when a basic part
of speech becomes an indicator of social trends.

The use of singular "they" comes with greater
recognition "they" refers to whose identities won't
conform to the binary of "he" or "she".
Gender-neutral pronoun for those who don't.

Some people choose to use "they" and "them"
to embrace who they are inside and out.
Whatever makes the individual happy.
"They" can be helpful if one is in doubt.

Political word of the year is "quid pro quo".
"Hot girl summer" is slang of the year.
Never heard of this slang word.
"Quid pro quo"could impeach Trump I hear.

Existential is 2019 Word of the Year
relating to existence, asking big questions
as we face our purpose, planetary challenges
we'd better be listening to suggestions.

The word for 2020 is yet to be chosen.
As the year unfolds we will see what fits.
First week is a tad unsettling, rattlings of war.
Hope we make choices where everyone benefits.

Dancing With the Corvallis Stars

Local dancers from non-profits paired
with pros to compete for their organization
and for the glitzy mirror ball. All donations
and entrance fees go to their causes.

The MC Alex was from the Utah Ballroom
Dance Company which also provided
the pros for six Corvallis earnest volunteer dancers.
The teachers had five hours to work with students.

The three judges were also local and appeared
to be competent and scored close to each other.
Some scores were generous, but they counted
effort and personality. All dancers did well.

The troop had three men and five women.
The female pros danced better than the men.
Also true of the local men. Some were not
the body type to be a dancer–but they tried.

They added audience votes, dancer fund-raising
and judges scores to determine the winner.
Audience voted during intermission. The second
half was the pros dancing–swing, theater arts,

Viennese Waltz, foxtrot, cha cha in glittery
costumes and exhibiting their showmanship.
The women outshined the men here as well.
They had a $1000 certificate for audience's favorite.

This prize was donated by a local market. The
same woman won both prizes. Kelly Volkmann,
dancing for School District theater programs,
outdanced Parks and Rec, DaVinci Days, the Arts Center,

Whiteside Theater, and Cornerstone Associates.
I saw the show in my wheelchair in the back row.
A friend I had not seen for awhile asked why I
wasn't out there dancing. Did I look like I was dancing?

My love for dance draws me to dance productions
in several venues. What a treat for the first time
we hosted pros and locals to dance for good causes.
I hope they do it again next year. My eyes will dance.

Figure Skating Competitions

The sport reveals diversity
with many nations.
Good to see.

So much skill, artistic grace,
brings some hope for the
human race.

I don't need numbers to show
their abilities,
glide and flow.

Liquid light, fluid
moves vivid.

Gymnasts

Bandaged limbs, braces, crutches—
some compete, endure
their clutches.

Glittery, skimpy, show clothes.
Strut their stuff, their flair.
Hair in bows.

Performances rated, compete
even after falls.
Hearts skip beat.

When they're in their groove,
they send love.

Ancient Stone Monument Builders

High tech buildings endure.
Who really built them?
We're not sure.

How did civilizations
know how to create
sensations?

They left no clues, advanced tools.
Precise, amazing–
where're their schools?

These ancient builders
bewilder.

Ancient Ooparts

Out of place artifacts are
not where they should be.
From the stars?

The more we explore the past,
we find new unknowns.
Theories blast.

Keep an open mind to finds.
Debate origins.
Science grinds.

Welcome a surprise
I'd surmise?

Coronavirus

Coronavirus' climbing,
circling the whole globe.
Bad timing.

Many deaths are due to it.
But the flus kill more.
Few knew it.

Masks worn in public protect
spread of illness—
few infect

as viruses, flus
bring sad news.

Make Some Noise

Applaud, protest, shout.
It's what humans are
all about.

Express loudly for equal rights.
Stand tall and firmly.
Expose plights.

Some nuisance noise is absurd.
Sift out what's needed
and be heard.

Sort fakes from what's true.
Must redo.

What is Important?

How do we decide what is
more important?
Any quiz?

What higher goals should we set?
Are they reachable
or forget?

We must live whatever choice.
When to shut up or
raise your voice?

So many viewpoints clash.
Balderdash?

Seasonal Decorations Change

Winter holiday light decor
turns to love— Valentine's Day.
When I yearn for hearts once more
I finally put winter figures away.
       I mummy the creatures into box tomb.
       Rebirth others from their hibernation womb.

Turns to love–Valentine's Day
when rain and cold seek warmth.
Time to put red and white on display.
Time to redecorate home and hearth.
       I love to decorate for all seasons
       for affirming life and artistic reasons.

When I yearn for hearts once more
splayed on figures' clothes and wooden hearts,
they seem to speckle and sparkle their encore.
Their smiles, love messages- joy imparts.
       Freed from darkness now in light,
       they can share and bring loving insight.

I finally put winter figures away—
elves, snowfolks, Santas, reindeer—
colorful miniatures of the holiday
exit to reappear next year.
       So many Festivals of Light to celebrate.
       I like to join in and participate.

I mummy the creatures into box tomb
carefully put in place to deposit
with labeled headstone in bedroom,
into the vault which is my closet.
       They remain there mostly out of mind
       until they emerge again, hard to find.

Rebirth others from their hibernation womb
is the task I completed–their resurrection.
Time for the hearts to shine and bloom.
Time for others to enjoy my collection.
       Each exchange brings new delight
       when it's their time in the spotlight.

Snowflakes

I look forward to the day when a snowflake can be a snowflake again.
Kenneth G. Libbrecht

Students
create snowflakes
made of cut white paper,
dangle them in windows to dream
of snow.

When snow
comes and shoveled
less allure, but can ski,
sled, snowboard, snowfolk, snowballs and
angels.

Snowflakes'
shape depends on
varied temperatures
and humidity zones— single ice
crystals.

Eighty
variant shapes:
needle, column, plate, rime.
Appear white, pure ice from color
spectrum.

Snowflakes
slang refers to
inflated uniqueness,
sense of entitlement and alt-right—
a slur.

Snowflake
generation,
political insult,
easily offended, differ
when deal.

Snowflakes
are beautiful.
Why defile nature's gift?
Just let snowflakes be snow crystals
again.

The Weathercasters

In exercise class sweating in their paraphernalia,
elderly jocks complain about wind, chill and rain.
With all their equipment and regalia
they undergo body complaints amid warmer terrain.
       In Oregon this time of year
       such comments tend to appear.

Elderly jocks complain about wind, chill and rain.
Hair-tossed, damp they count their moves.
I view such evaluations inane
when they spout whatever behooves
       them to state this distraction.
       More climate change inaction?

With all their equipment and regalia
they fight fat and tussle
with images and nostalgia
as they try to strengthen muscle.
       No music, the same routine.
       No wonder they drift to another scene.

They undergo body complaints amid warmer terrain
when I mention the intense Australian fires.
They are lucky to be here, it is plain.
They need a new perspective our future requires.
       You can be fit, but it is all for naught,
       if the world's polluted beyond what it ought.

In Oregon this time of year,
cheer on the green and cleansing air.
Snowstorms are rarely seen here.
We have better weather than elsewhere.
       Nature is taking us on a wild ride.
       Hold on, help out, be on Greta's side.

Such comments tend to appear
because we face change and uncertainty.
We perceive darkness and fear.
Pain seems to last an eternity.
       So as the class grunts and groans–
       I'll try compassion for our moans.

Exercising with Grace

Off count, off rhythm, off motion
the elderly, mostly awkward
exercisers rely on grace (not
in actions) to get them through.

They help each other with
equipment, greet each other
warmly, but as athletes?
Most are not very graceful.

Way beyond my dancing days,
I do not expect my achy,
arthritic body to be graceful,
but I admire classmates' attempts.

Some are woefully out of step
and their agility greatly compromised.
Many are hindered by injuries, decline,
fogginess and pain. But they persist.

Some adapt routines to their
waning abilities and watch others
struggle to figure it all out. Grace
can be bestowed to their spirit?

Perhaps the goal is not gracefulness
but healthy movements. Today
I wonder if I achieve either. Yep,
today is just not my day to shine.

Persistent Clingers

Someone told me our bodies age,
we lose our youthful vigor because
we would not want to leave Earth.

If we did not age we would reproduce
too many to sustain the planet.
By now we would balloon into gadzillions.

What mechanisms would we devise to die?
Wars, viruses, run out of resources?
When would be the limits to growth?

We have unintentional, accidental deaths,
natural disasters to cull a few. Do we need
to nix uncontrolled breeding to the mix?

Who would decide when we have enough people,
resources, other fauna and flora and how
would we get rid of the excess?

Barring unforeseen illnesses and death,
we try to plan our lives knowing we face a deadline
and life here is temporary, no matter in what shape.

Many people try all kinds of techniques to cling
to life: transfer consciousness to robots, "cloud"
for later transfer, freeze to unthaw in the future.

Maybe the future will not come with the technology
to make these provisions work. People cling to the hope
there is a heaven, another incarnation elsewhere.

Perhaps it is fear of the unknown that keep people
in the gym, on diets and meds, anything to cling
to a functional body in a dysfunctional world.

Aging can be a painful, disabling process. No wonder
people escape pain any way they can. All we can do
is cling to the good things and stand up against the bad.

We are going to go somewhere, someday. Until then,
just do the best we can to hedge our bets.
Cling to love, peace, happiness, kindness.

Kicking It with Boots Riley

Art can end up answering questions or asking questions. But when it's not
connected to actual movements, it doesn't ask the right questions. Boots Riley

Boots Riley was the Martin Luther King Jr. Day speaker
at Oregon State University's largest auditorium. We had
no idea who he was and what a conversation with him entailed.
Our son was on the local MLK Jr. Board for a while so we went
to support the great programs they did for King's birthday. Our son
had heard him before, so did not go. Clueless, we went.

Hundreds poured in. Many from the graduate students union.
I thought the 48 year old Black rapper, producer, screenwriter,
film director and activist was going to introduce his film,
"Sorry to Bother You." But an hour in, I realized he was here
to discuss his work for unions, to reduce wealth inequity,
to suggest methods to achieve a revolution for worker's rights.

The audience clicked their fingers or clapped when they liked
his comments. He was pretty mellow for a radical. His ideas
for cultural change urged group action. Boycotting companies
by our purchases is not enough. We need to kick some butts.
But he is not into violence. His film sounds rather surreal. He was
speaking to an agreeing crowd and gave a history of activism.

I found his conversation interesting. I do not have the mobility
or energy for the activism needed. But I can write, march, ask
and encourage questioning, support positive causes. I write
to promote awareness and raise questions. Each individual must
choose what their consciousness needs to grow and create change.
We would not be here if all was well? But why still so oppressive?

Slip knowledge into entertainment. You can't change minds with a heavy hand.
Preachy movies or lousy beats don't move hearts or feet. Because if you truly
want revolution, you've got to move to get it. Boots Riley

Who Will Step Up?

I
can't
change the
world myself.
I need so much help.
We will need everyone on board.

There's
good
and bad
fires. Burn
wisely in control.
Indigenous people do.

The
air
must clean
for life to
breathe healthily. Air
keeps us alive or air kills us.

Seas
are
poisoned,
plasticized.
Water polluted.
A life necessity is spoiled.

Land
is
mined,
resources
exploited. People
die from few greedy profiteers.

Where
to
turn for
survival?
Can activists act
in time to save from extinction?

Small Walls

Small
walls
in our
yard hold back
small slopes, brace the ground.
Moss greens concrete chunks to match grass.

Small
walls
built chunk
by chunk to
divide, separate
designed to keep us safe, alone?

Small
walls
between
people are
better than tall walls—
if you can see through–not solid.

Tall
walls
create
boundaries— seesaws
at the border between
slats so children play on both sides.

Tall
walls
tumble
in Berlin.
Rubble removed so
people cross freely–there not here.

Masks

Around
the world people
wear masks to prevent flu
or air pollution, cleanse air for
breathing.

During
protests tear gas,
smoky missiles tossed at
police. Riot gear is needed
for all.

Daily
like Halloween
or a masked ball disguise
at the mall, anywhere at all-
don masks.

Masks worn
to conceal who
does not want to be seen,
identified with violent cause–
danger.

Bare-faced
we mask truth to
deceive and protect
what we feel we must hide, also
mislead.

Masks
in medicine
or the lab might help us.
Masks as cover-ups for a good
purpose?

Reversing Migration

There are
days when I wish
my grandparent stayed
in or I could return to their
Sweden.

I tend
to favor Swedish
ways of thinking, designs
for living and progress, treating
others.

Swedes gave
us Greta to
lead us to a future,
to take sustainable action.
Save us?

Right new
I would go there,
for my actions here aren't
effective in this negative
climate.

We face
global shifts as
migrants seek better lives.
My ancestors did just that, but
dreams die.

Where are
we headed? Where
can we go to for peace?
Age leaves me little time to make
a change.

A Special Day

Today
is Groundhog Day.
Punxsutawney Phil will
look for his shadow for spring
to start.

He is
right only
thirty-nine or forty
percent of the time. Correct for
somewhere?

Today
is Super Bowl.
I'll be at gymnastics
match— less violent, less risky
pastime.

Also
this special day—
02.02 2020
is a rare palindrome for new
decade.

Lots of
discoveries
and more hopes for today.
Let's give this new year and decade
a chance?

Watching the Super Bowl

Kansas City Chiefs beat San Francisco 49'ers.

I
had
never
watched football's
Super Bowl–so weird.
Dislike the violence, concussions.
No fan.

I
still
prefer
basketball.
Women get more press.
Getting more equity but still
less pay.

Three
of
us watched.
Two had no clue what
rules were. We laughed a lot. No one
too hurt.

I
still
enjoy
gymnastics.
figure skating, the Olympics
and dance

My
poor
husband
patiently
tried to explain the game.
I just like it when they throw ball
and run.

I
think
football
players get
paid much too much and
women get underpaid still in
all sports.

I
don't
like the
collisions.
Seems unnecessary
to cause such injuries for just
football.

I
don't
think I
will watch the
Super Bowl or
any football game again for
too dark.

I
did
not care
who won. It's
too brutal —massive
jocks in tight paints, padded shoulders,
helmets.

All
the
glitz at
half time to
divert, attention
from gladiators with skimpy dressed
women.

136

The Polar Plunge
    Fundraiser for Special Olympics Benefit

Over
seven hundred
people volunteered to
get donations for the polar
plunge. Brrr.

They are
like lemmings who
race to the water this
time in the rain while wearing a
costume.

Fifty
teams dressed as trolls,
Thor, Spider Girl, Super
heroes, Maleficent, Elsa from
Frozen.

Our son
for charity
dressed as a pirate to
plunge into a frigid river.
Shiver.

We had
breakfast before
the event—warm quiches.
His parents wondered how he'd change
wet clothes.

They have
change tents, still cold.
Then the long drive home chilled.
All for a good cause. I'd rather
donate.

His Dad
went to see the
chilly polar plunge, but
Mom stayed home warm, a cold plunging
coward.

Parents
try to support,
their children, but I doubt
freezing's part of the deal? I hope
it's not.

But we're
proud our son cares
for others to such lengths.
My parents would just think I am
crazy.

Sifting the News

As I
peruse the news,
I glaze over the bad,
cling to the good, hopeful signs we'll
survive.

Painful
images are
hard to ignore and sear,
into my heart and soul can not
bear it.

On screen
a click and gone,
out of sight if not mind.
Computer blinks out like on my
TV.

Shifting
vision and some
channels, turning the page,
are ways to deal with what terror
brings us.

How do
we help? Hinder
by denial? Action
must be taken? But by whom? Or
by me?

I do
what I can to
cope and act, but pain holds
mobility, ways for me to
move on.

Retreat
to unknowing?
Sift and shift what I can?
Heaviness darkens. Please sustain
the light.

Coronavirus Panic

The virus is rapidly spreading
across the globe in unusual places.
Panicky people are dreading
going into public spaces.
        Masks and gloves are worn,
        to protect for a virus— airborne.

Across the globe in unusual places,
with unknown carriers,
humanity is not sure what it faces.
Knock down information barriers.
        The data is either concealed or fake.
        What kind of protections can we take?

Panicky people are dreading
impacts on health and economy.
What puzzling path are we treading?
Faith in divine or astronomy?
        Quarantines don't control
        the viral spread or patrol.

Going into public places
can be hazardous to your health,
a threat to all countries and races,
impacting commerce and wealth.
        How can we protect one another?
        How many dreams will we smother?

Masks and gloves are worn.
Wash hands often and prepare
to stock up necessities officials warn
as people become more aware.
        A global pandemic underway?
        Where will the virus stay away?

To protect from a virus airborne
in polluted, crowded conditions,
leaves populace anxious and forlorn.
How many more viral renditions?
        Now wait and see what's to come?
        Any relief would be welcome.

All is Well

All is well. Everything is working out for my highest good. Out of this situation only good can come. Louise Hay.

Make Hay when the sun shines optimist?
A cloudy, gloomy kind?
I'm murky in the mist,
my highest path yet to find.
    She may be right, who can tell?
    For some, this attitude is a hard sell.

A cloudy, gloomy, sort
awaiting the sun?
What is your best resort?
Has a pessimist won?
    How much free will can we exert?
    How many do we unwillingly hurt?

I'm murky in the mist,
hard to see clearly when in pain.
I try to persist and resist
for something upbeat to remain.
    Choose light over dark innate?
    Same with love over hate?

My highest path yet to find?
Will I discover it by journey's end?
Unknowing fills my probing mind.
What is the potential dividend?
    All is well is hard to see
    when surrounded by misery.

She may be right, who can tell?
I continue to delve into life's mystery.
I certainly hope all is well.
Any guidance for my inquiry?
    I'd like to believe as she did.
    How much are events fluid?

For some this attitude is a hard sell.
Oblivious? Insightful? A better idea?
Somewhere their trust and confidence fell?
We're flooded with options on media.
    Are we part of some cosmic plan?
    Are we doing the best we can?

Atoning for Flyskam

Flyskam
is Swedish
for the flight emissions
environmental concern or
flight shame.

Buying
carbon offsets
reduces people's guilt
when need to fly. Flyers beware
of scams.

Utes in
Colorado
capture the natural
methane gas then makes energy
to use.

Coldplay
cancelled World Tour
because of flying's
environmental concerns and
impact.

Choose
airlines who
support projects to help
planet— globally planting trees
projects.

Websites
like Cool Effect or
Green-E or Gold Standard
to learn of programs, buy carbon
offsets.

Travel
apps like Hopper
donate trees from booking
services. Reforestation
worldwide.

Skip your
flight plans if they're
un-necessary. It
will help, but just part of job- all
pitch in.

Climate
Action Reserve
a registry for offset
projects to track, ensure they do
their claims.

Trees are
slow growing, so
long before tree pulls
much carbon from the air. But still
plant trees.

Carbon
Offsetting and
Reduction scheme for
International Aviation
in place.

Flyskam
can increase our
progress to clean up our
act into action for the health
of all.

I have
given up flights.
Germy, crunched, bad food,
my wheelchair cumbersome. My guilt
assuaged.

Many ways
to help planet.
Time is running out.
Trees can't do it all. We can do it
faster.

Skin

Why
is
color
a problem?
Diversity is
beautiful and treat to eyes.

The
past
racist,
cultural
stupidities should
be eliminated by now.

Based
on
power
struggles, old
outworn beliefs and
changes in outlook and justice.

What
should
be focus
is each
one's character and
how they serve others with respect.

Who
cares
about one's
color if
one loves anyone?
Color is a prism of light and joy.

Difference

God just makes some people different. Joshua Bennett

Some claim we are all unique
with different talents and flaws.
Humans often raise my pique,
some make my contemplation pause.
      We dismiss flaws as being human.
      We often lack restraint and acumen.

With different talents and flaws
we bumble through our lives,
tend to fumble earth-bound laws.
Not everyone strives and thrives.
      Capacities differ, we can't keep pace
      with the challenges of the human race.

Humans often raise my pique
with their tendency toward violence.
With division reaching its peak,
we become cocooned in silence.
      Facing a dire situation
      humans might try cooperation.

Some make my contemplation pause.
I admit I become judgmental
when humans hurt and war because
they differ on what's fundamental.
      We've had so long if we do evolve,
      so many conundrums yet to solve.

We dismiss flaws as being human.
"Boys will be boys". "They don't know better"
'They are doing the best they can."
"Some are not born to follow the letter."
      Excuses humans make for their misdeeds,
      inequities, exclusions, ignoring other's needs.

We often lack restraint or acumen.
Extreme beliefs bring grief and tension.
Globally the mistreatment of children and women,
lead to abuses too horrible to mention.
      Humans need an upgrade, a tweak of DNA
      if we are a species that deserves to stay.

Political Climate

There is only one way we're going to change
our political climate and ensure we establish
some respect in our discourse and that is
to show there is a real price to pay for being
a disrespectful, partisan idiot.

Mark McKinnon

How Much Do We Need to Know?

With media blasting the "fake" and "real" news—
screens in hands, before our eyes.
Radios blare additional clues.
We are open to deceit and surprise.
        Tune in or tune out?
        Ignore or shout?

Screens in hands, before our eyes—
images embed, cause distress.
For some a lucrative enterprise
at the expense of others for success.
        Meditate in a quiet place
        to escape the rat race?

Radios blare additional clues.
You can imagine what you hear.
Many ideas just enhance our blues.
We hope for the horizon to clear.
        Do we take a chill pill?
        Dismay at Capitol Hill?

We are open to deceit and surprise.
Retreat to privacy and silence?
Any hope for compromise?
Wait for a time of resilience?
        Events happen unlike things before.
        What alternatives can we explore?

Tune in or tune out?
Curiosity compels me to be aware.
Hope for a turnabout?
When weary, I tune out–but I care,
        so I listen as long as I can.
        I want to be a partisan.

Ignore or shout?
Too angry to ignore I must act.
Action is what change is all about.
It's very hard not to react.
        Use technology with care.
        Consider what you want to share.

Boundaries

Many boundaries do not have walls,
see-through or closed fences to define
when to intervene in someone's squalls,
when you might have crossed the line.
>Unseen boundaries are hard to detect.
>When is too much interference or neglect?

See-through or closed fences to define
territory do not defer all who intrude.
Boundaries crossed when intent does not align
with those we do not want to include.
>Sometimes we are clueless how we hurt.
>Our consciousness needs a growth spurt.

When to intervene in someone's squalls
requires wisdom to know what to do.
Sometimes we have to show some balls,
some persistence to follow through.
>Boundaries to protect or limit access?
>When do we know if they were a success?

When you might have crossed the line,
chances of healing diminish.
Communication tends to decline.
Sometimes you cannot repair or finish.
>Wounded, depressed or bleeding—
>symptoms of what one is needing.

Unseen boundaries are hard to detect.
A predator is too focused on its prey.
Some people show no respect
and allow no one to stand in their way.
>Boundaries sadly are punctured and broken,
>by violent actions and when one has misspoken.

When is too much interference or neglect?
National boundaries are futile when global action
is needed to makes changes and to reflect.
We need connection and interaction.
>Sometimes I erect boundaries to protect my heart.
>It is hard to witness darkness and stand apart.

Selecting Presidential Candidates

The
slow
process
for choosing
is annoying and
plagued by rumors, miscounts, attacks.

Why
not
one vote
same day for
all voters to choose.
No buying fickle electorate.

All
this
fuss and
divisive
politics for a
shorter bickering duration.

A
few
debates,
articles,
candidate's plans and
stance and their character revealed.

I
am
weary
of the race.
Any candidate
who can beat Trump, my chosen one.

Voting

If
we're
voting,
will our vote
count? Popular vote?
Electoral college is flawed.

If
we
are lead
by a few–
representative?
A just system? Need a revamp?

I
am
tired,
wary, mad.
No system can work?
Anyone care for justice or truth?

Impeachment
Republican senators block impeachment of Donald Trump

He's guilty some will admit.
Lack the courage.
They acquit.

Except the brave Senator Mitt.
Took off his gloves for
catcher's mitt.

Susan Collins is a twit.
Thinks he learned lesson.
Both dimwits.

Hard to garner some wit—
end of it.

Democratic Candidates

My indecision hems and haws.
Each candidate has
perceived flaws.

But none as bad as Donald—
liar and bully,
brazen, fraud.

Any Democrat will get
my vote and support-
no regret.

We need hope, problem solver
not mad, mess maker -
resolver.

Get us out of slump.
Dump the rump.

Postcards to the President

On March 15th, the Ides of March,
non-fans of the president
will bombard the White House
with protest postcards.

Since they will not bolster his ego
he will never see the avalanche,
the nationwide effort to let him know
many people are not Trump-bots.

He does not read, but maybe his staff
like in Congress, tally the pro and cons
people send on issues–don't dare tell him.

Our Huddle group from the Women's March
called Writing the Wrongs to Rights
are a bunch of older women writer/
activists who persist and resist Trump.

Pens and postcards sprawl over a table.
We encircle the task, complete with stamps.
We rant and laugh, share funny video clips
from cell phones- like a goat nurses a horse.

A cat nurses ducklings. We are not nursing
Trump. Some writers quartered pink cover
stock to send him pink slips and wrote the
reason for his firing. Some just said "You're fired."

Just during this session we wrote over 100
postcards and plan to write more. One member
took several batches of cards to mail in a bunch.
She plans to call our local paper to cover the project.

We are all weary of having to sign petitions
and the pleas for donations, to witness Trump
overthrow of law, democracy, the environment.

We are having to support his expensive golf trips,
plane pollution, lawsuits against the attacks on all
fronts by his administration. Are we too old for this?

Most of us will be at the March 8th Women's March
at the Capital–joining compassionate people, who
want to improve and better the world, not destroy it.

Protest Postcards

Protest
postcards get
mailed today to Trump.
Across nation people say "you're
fired".

Despite
quarantines they
mail cards for Trump's
Ides of March, hope he will change and
listen

He does
not read, but can't
ignore avalanche to
inform him many don't support
conduct.

His lack
of leadership
imperils the planet.
Fair election seems just too
far off.

Where do
we turn for help?
News distorted, thwarted.
World-wide, heavy, bully's impact
is felt.

I'm too
impatient to
wait him out, as he stirs
global situation like a
warlock.

Precious
lives are at risk.
His arrogance could end
the world bloated, smug, self serving,
nutcase.

Postcards to Trump
March 15, 2000

Opposers of Trump–non-fans,
will swamp White House with
other plans.

With justice still out of reach
Congress divided
to impeach,

democracy believers
send post cards as stress
relievers.

He'll never see them:
panned item.

Thersitical Trump

Thersitical: scurrilous, foulmouthed, grossly abusive. Word of the Day

Trump is
an example
of the term he'll not read,
spell, accept because of his big
ego.

Trump is
a bully and
predator, self-engrossed,
gross in many ways, endangers
the world.

Trump makes
me fearful, mad
at power grabs, evil
intentions, duped Trumpbots who
follow.

We can't
vote him out with
Electoral College for
it is outdated and biased.
Now hacked?

Dire
challenges face
the world with few leaders
we trust to act on our planet's
behalf.

The Rockets Red Glare

The rockets red glare,
the bombs bursting in air
gave proof to the world
that USA better beware.

Our incompetent President
killed an Iranian general without precedent,
setting up another middle-east war.
He should be mental hospital or jail resident.

Let's impeach the son of a bitch,
scratch out his negative itch.
We must stop him in time,
seek peace. Time to switch.

With climate change and poor wealth distribution
we all must make a positive contribution.
Can we wait for justice? Voting too late?
We need leaders with a sustaining attribute.

Will rational minds prevail?
Will we survive to tell the tale?
The world's angry and suffering.
Are we doomed to weep and wail?

Instability is not the fault of one man
but he is doing all he can
to unstabilize, threaten our survival.
What is his ultimate plan?

We become stunned and numb
under his rule of thumb.
We cannot predict his actions.
Any solutions welcome.

The rockets red glare
the bombs bursting in air
gave warning to the world
the USA is not aware?

Another March

Tomorrow we prepare to march again.
Recent march was to impeach
another wayward policy causing pain.
Our president tends to overreach.
	Empower the people of the Earth
	against leaders of little worth.

Recent march was to impeach.
Women, LGBTQ and racial issues
seek justice when boundaries breech,
prey to predatory actions and views.
	How long must the old hierarchies rule?
	Is marching our only tool?

Another wayward policy causing pain
sends people into the streets.
Must we march, try to restrain?
How many replays and repeats?
	We've polluted minds, land, water, air.
	So much urgency to become aware.

Our president tends to over-reach
our Constitution and global restrictions.
Should it be up to each
of us to oppose his warped depictions
	of what is fair and just?
	He has lost our trust.

Empower the people of the Earth
who seek peace, justice and common ground,
work for renewal and planet's rebirth.
Cooperate together or woes will compound.
	Everywhere inequities prevail.
	More leaders should be in jail.

Against leaders of little worth
a vote in a rigged, outdated election system
will not bring change or unearth
deep seated problems whose origins stem
	from abuse of power and greed.
	How do we deliver the methods we need?

Marching Against the Mythomane

Mythomane: a person with a strong or irresistible propensity for fantasizing, lying or exaggeration. Dictionary.com

Calling
Trump mythomane
kindest term to describe
not popularly voted for
leader.

Women
will march again
to oppose performance
of this Twitterpated, fake news
buffoon.

Around
the country we
endure winter weather–
on January 18th
to march.

Almost
started World War.
A delusional man
who is unfit for serving our
nation.

If we
impeach him we
get Pence. Not much better.
But seems sane, if devious, not Trump
at least.

So on
Saturday I
will join angry marchers,
for peace, cooperation,
justice

We don't.
need predator
empowered to act for
our country's best interests or for
our lives.

Under the Gazebo

2020 Women's March Central Park, Corvallis, Oregon 10:30-11:30

My husband and I have been under-prepared
for several marches. It took me hours to thaw
after last march in a wheelchair. But this time
we had umbrella, poncho, layers of clothing, gloves,
signs. I wore my pink hat, red scarf, three layers
of sweatshirts, coat and poncho–even lap blanket.

We left early expecting a large crowd
and we wanted to park near the park.
They did not set up any audio equipment.
The publicity was poor, but where was everyone?
A few came and left until 20 diehards gathered
under the gazebo–out of the drizzle.

We were to be part of a national march
as we had been other years. I wanted
to support the new more diverse leadership.
Those who stayed were one Asian, four men,
some from Albany, Harrisburg, Monmouth, and
Newport. One heard about the march from NPR,
Thought on Progressives and NOW websites,
some found it hard to find. Maybe they went elsewhere,

We gathered in a circle, under cover and
introduced ourselves and why we were here.
No students and no one under age 50.
Many retired. All united against Trump
and his policies on treatment of women,minorities,
healthcare, immigration, environment. All
wanted to get out the vote and engage drop-outs
and young voters to vote. All angry at our situation.
All dedicated activists, marchers. Most had signs.
Mine was laminated: Time's up Trump Time to Go!

Each of the articulate attendees believed
we have to stand up, be active for change
any way we can. Many did community work.
Several mentioned they were doing this
for their grandchildren. Even though the ERA
just passed, women's empowerment was
an urgent issue for all. Recent progress
still has along way to go. We took a group picture,
then dispersed from our personalized, intimate march.

Thawing

Leaving the Women's March
in cold, light rain, even though
I was under cover of a gazebo,
layered under a poncho, I was chilled.

Both my husband and I had cold
hands and feet. We drove through
a fast food drive-thru en route home.
I clutched the warm food bag.

After lunch I worked on the computer
which warmed my hands. After a nap I
could go stocking-footed. I was thawing.
2020 is the centennial of women getting to vote.

Hopefully passing ERA will not be challenged.
We should not have to wait for men to give
us our human rights. I have not chilled my anger.
Around the world the few control the majority.

Seems I am always thawing from a dark, cold,
world. Will I get so red hot mad, my burning
will thaw my frozen fear? We march despite
preaching to the choir, to ignite hope.

Divisions on Display

Marches and rallies for anti-abortion, pro-choice,
gun controls or not, pro or anti-Trump.
Climate change activists, deniers give voice.
Divisions on opposite sides tend to clump.
>Black lives matter, women's rights too.
>Protesters shouting what to do.

Gun controls or not, pro-or anti-Trump,
impeach or not. Vote party over nation?
Candidates hope their standings jump.
Few unite about any situation.
>Caps and handmaiden's tale garb.
>Some carry signs with a stinging barb.

Climate change activists, deniers give choice
feed need over greed. Wealth inequity won
over planet's health. Youth serve an invoice.
So much activism to get their goals done.
>Imagine the power if we acted together
>for freedom, to prepare for changing weather.

Divisions on opposite sides tend to clump.
Little listening, lots of anger over events.
Plastic turns oceans into garbage dump.
We plasticize while no action prevents
>stopping and acting while we can.
>We must develop a global plan.

Black lives matter, women's rights too—
all beings need our nurture.
Too much power to too few.
We face an inequitable, polluted future.
>Find unity to work for our survival.
>Cooperate, don't blame our rival.

Protestors shouting what to do.
Moderates pressured to take sides.
Anti-any group— find a breakthrough.
Enhance unity not what divides.
>Violence, hateful confrontations
>are infecting many nations.

Annuities

People always live forever when there is any annuity to be paid them.
Jane Austen in Sense and Sensibility

When we
talk of having
guaranteed minimum
incomes for all, will we all live
longer?

Perhaps
less homeless
and more comfortable?
Special upgrades and more gifts for
purchase?

Fair shake,
distribution
of wealth handled better?
Less hazardous work choices will
compete?

Choices
enhanced, people
live lives- any length- better?
Afford to sustain ourselves and
planet?

We have
billions of
people to care for. Do we
have the will? Can we all find the
best way?

Scar Across Our Heart

New wall built in Organ Pipe National Monument on Tohono Oodham Nation land. "We are enduring crimes against humanity...This wall is already putting a scar across our heart." Verlon M. Jose.

Cactus
tumble, blasted,
protected cactuses
sacrificed to build wall— Trump's wall
faster.

Once an
oasis and
aquifer, burial
ground for Tohono Oodham,
now wall.

They axed
saguaros near
the wall by the southwest
border to prevent migrants to
pass through.

Natives'
reservation breeched.
Tribal people live near
Organ Pipe Monument and are
angry.

It is
a UNESCO
biosphere reserve. So
why are we building a Trump wall
through it?

Border
control claims the
unhealthy cactuses
destroyed, others are relocated
elsewhere.

Rumors
persist on both sides.
Destroying sacred sites
is an international crime
as well.

A gash
through middle of
of this revered desert
contains remains of downed
cactus.

Native lands
also have some
petroglyphs and rock art.
Wall is a desecration and
attack.

No laws
protecting land.
Laws waived to expedite
evolutionary change of
landscape.

Species
endangered, not
protected. This push is
contrast to previous border
projects.

They hope
oasis can
be saved, taken from
the Natives before Organ Pipe
was built.

Workers
found old bones as
pump water, endanger
sonoya mud turtles, nearby
people.

Anger
has spread around
the country to Congress.
The tragedy continues— a Trump
hot mess.

The Women in White

A woman enters her husband's house wearing white and leaves his house wearing white. Local Afghan saying.

The latter white refers to burial wraps,
another abused wife, killed by her husband.
One way to break free of these traps,
find way to kill him, freed from his demand.
   Prison is freedom for these women.
   No laws protect women before they kill men.

Another abused wife, killed by her husband.
A teenage bride married to an older man.
Raped, stabbed, shot, tortured, no reprimand
for the perpetrator, no release from this plan.
   Some act when men attack the children.
   Women can no longer tolerate abuse then.

One way to break free of these traps
is as a murderer in handcuffs.
Unenforced laws could help, perhaps.
Now safer in prison, than legal and cultural scuffs.
   Children with them until age 8,
   then they are taken to educate.

Find ways to kill him, freed from his demand
to be subservient and his demented masculinity.
Despite new laws on paper and UN in hand,
culture does not support equality or divinity
   that is not a male hierarchy.
   Women suffer from this malarkey.

Prison is freedom for these women.
Prisons staffed by women fare best.
Any hope for change? A positive omen?
Follow-through on abuse, violence, contest
   the cultural traditions that allow this to persist?
   Give women the power and access to resist?

No laws protect women before they kill men.
Wives are left to themselves to protect their family.
Women are not an equal citizen.
This is the reason for the homily.
   A women enters and leaves husband's home in white.
   Women unite and prepare for justice to right.

Women's Rights Without Barriers

Globally there is an increase in femicide,
exploitation, harassment from oppressive patriarchy.
More deaths from despair and suicide
as women confront a male hierarchy.
>   Women are manipulated pawns,
>   weeded like dandelions from our lawns.

Exploitation, harassment from oppressive patriarchy
suppresses women's human rights.
Out-dated, cultural malarkey
adds to their suffering, dangerous plights.
>   Water cannons, tear gas, arrests and stones
>   faced as they march in strident tones.

More deaths from despair and suicide
are preventable if equity becomes reality.
The impacts for justice could be felt world-wide,
if people respected everyone and peace was an actuality.
>   Woman are more likely to be limited and poor-
>   pelted, withered flowers their metaphor.

As women confront a male hierarchy
they become more empowered, stand tall.
They broaden safety and opportunity
for the benefit of us all.
>   Men should cherish women who gave them birth,
>   share resources and enhance their self-worth.

Women are manipulated pawns
man-handled by fear and violence.
Resist until a new day dawns
and emerge from imposed silence.
>   If humanity can improve
>   it will come with cooperation and love.

Weeded like dandelions from our lawns,
borne by puffs to seed bright, sun-spots,
women remain unfulfilled until hope spawns
to eliminate barriers, share the slots.
>   Why are men so regressive?
>   Why are men violent and possessive?

Bias Against Women

UN study shows 90% of women and men globally have a bias against women.

With 50% of the world's population women
this percentage is offensive.
This presents a gloomy omen
for women seeking equality, defensive.
>Come on women wake up, stand tall.
>Don't accept Old World Order's protocol.

This percentage is offensive.
Women suffer cultural oppression
Why aren't women more pensive?
Fight back to end their suppression?
>In this world of abuse and violence,
>we need more people to break the silence.

This presents a gloomy omen.
Too many believe in male hierarchy.
How do we melt the hearts of snowmen.
Will a New World Order find the key?
>All the young girls' find dreams thwarted,
>watch male power as opportunities sorted.

Women seeking equality and defensive
of their human rights,
find wealth inequities are expensive
to disenfranchised, increase their plights.
>Women suffer disproportionally.
>Children see this pattern unfortunately.

Come on women wake up stand tall
Take actions to improve women's lives.
Improve conditions that appall.
Increase chances humanity survives.
>Woman power makes a berth
>for everyone to know their worth.

Don't accept Old World Orders' protocol.
Help with humanity's ascension.
When will new intentions install?
Do we have to rise to a 5th dimension?
>The lives of women too often depress
>and lack access to express.

International Women's Day
March 8th 2020

Around the world women march and protest
treatment of women— lack of equity, abuse.
Some places they face arrest,
attacked by traditions, archaic, obtuse.
> Equality for women still distant.
> Globally women remain vigilant.

Treatment of women–lack of equity, abuse,
denies education, opportunities, self-empowerment.
Poverty, discrimination, violence no excuse
for this in a "woke" world. No wonder women resent
> loss of control over own bodies, limited future,
> at the whim of an oppressive culture.

Some places they face arrest,
pelted by shoes and stones.
Men launch counter marches, think they know best.
No way this behavior atones.
> Why don't they share with sisters and mothers?
> Why do they support their fathers and brothers?

Attacked by traditions archaic, obtuse-
nations tax sanitary products. Scotland gives them for free.
Period Pad Protests, menstruation fears produce
lack of chances for changes toward equity.
> Gender gap in economics has stagnated.
> UN Study says results show less progress than anticipated.

Equality for women still distant
despite many benefits women bring to the table.
Male power structures are still resistant.
Women can't achieve what they are able.
> Blocked by challenges unjust and unfair.
> Predatory men better become aware.

Globally women remain vigilant,
angry, insist on their human rights.
Despite setbacks, women remain persistent.
When will we unite to address their plights?
> Change repressive laws, outdated constitutions,
> biased institutions. Time for retributions?

Spiritual Climate

Culture values are in themselves,
neutral as well as universal
and as much depends how individuals
and ethnic groups use them.
Values are influenced by so many factors
such as geography, climate, religion,
the economy and technology.

F. Sionil Jose

When Are We Lost?

You can never be lost on your path, because your karmic way is always unfolding or revealing before you–it is the red threat of destiny, and it's impossible for you to miss anything you need to do or experience, anyone you need to meet or be with, anything you're here to understand.   Sara Wiseman

If the universe guides you–just chill?
What if this incarnation is not a good path?
What if you're like Sisyphus falling back down the hill?
What if you dislike the aftermath?
        What if you want to change course?
        What if you have no recourse?

What if this incarnation is not a good path.
Maybe your life chart imprinted the wrong code?
What if you are not an empath?
What if you took on an overload?
        If destiny's set, are we a cosmic puppet?
        What if you decide to up it?

What if you're like Sisyphus falling back down the hill?
You are not interested to climb to the top.
Is there such a thing as free will?
How can you make this re-creating pain stop?
        What is the point of all this debating?
        Why are we stuck–waiting?

What if you dislike the aftermath?
Fell into the wrong crowd?
A violent killer? A sociopath?
Certainly not a life to be proud.
        Why not just peace, joy and light?
        Why all the darkness in our plight?

What if you want to change course?
Destiny's set, who writes the script? Who Is the puppeteer?
Can we pause to reflect and find new resource?
We are integrating what's happened? Becomes clear?
        In a state of waiting we can feel lost?
        I'm feeling manipulated and bossed.

What if you have no recourse?
We are part of an evolving cosmic plan?
Only an illusion for better or worse?
Carry on the best we can?
        If we are a cosmic puppet,
        I'd like to be a muppet.

Belief in Winged Beings

Winged-ones human, animal,
supernatural,
or angel–

wings uplift our spirit, mind.
Whether true or not,
a good find.

We take flight without our woes.
Imagine a light realm.
Cosmos flows.

Do you need to know
it is so?

Predestination

Do we incarnate coded?
Free will just a hope?
Pre-loaded?

Synchronicities were planned?
Timing predestined?
Choice is banned?

Any say in life's mission?
Who decides and gives
permission?

Life like a dance card?
Disregard?

Bright Spots

Good-hearted avatars
nurture the planet—
human stars.

Cosmic light and energy
flow to us all in
synergy.

When all beings shine their light
with compassion,
we'll enlight.

Bright spots surround us.
They ground us.

The Year of the Collective Breakthrough

Interaction with self, with other human beings and with Nature, all should lead to harmony and peace. That's the purpose of life. Anand Damani

Sara Wiseman has some forecasts
for 2020. She suggests
the soul collective wakes up, casts
a "4" year of organization bequests.
   We manifest intention and breakthrough.
   We have work and building to do.

For 2020 she suggests
we dump the drama, inclusivity be the norm.
Illness in leaders dumps old. New requests
help Gaia to fix climate change impacts, inform
   us to shed darkness, drama and fear.
   Sounds like a promising year.

The soul collective wakes up, casts
focus on aliens and space travels,
more green inventions, greed blasts,
more action as our future unravels.
   We begin the Aquarian Age.
   Humanity is evolving into a new stage.

A "4" year of organization bequests
possibility we could get our stuff together.
Begin an era where we bring out our bests,
confront our polluted planet, decide whether
   we will be responsible and sustain
   a planet we have failed to maintain.

We manifest intention and breakthrough
old hierarchies which do not serve us.
Create new pathways, non-violently undo
behaviors that make us stressed and nervous.
   Can we uplift our vision?
   Make viability our mission?

We have work and building to do
in a cooperative, positive manner.
Give humanity and planet a clue?
Wave a cosmically-connected banner?
   We are part of a multiverse.
   Will we make it better or worse?

Half-way through Eclipse Gateway
New Moon Eclipse December 25th- Full Moon Eclipse January 10th 2019-2020

The new year and decade starts with predictions.
We are to release the old patterns for awareness and joy.
Ask questions, seek new prescriptions.
Powerful energy is here to employ.
Allow more of your truth to shine through.
Not an easy possibility to do.

We are to release the old patterns for awareness and joy.
Have you evolved a new perspective?
Can you manifest new experiences to deploy?
To cultivate joy, fulfillment, uplifts –are you receptive?
Can you be of service and contribute
to the world? Have love to distribute?

Ask questions, seek new prescriptions.
You cannot see the whole pathway.
Ponder and wonder about new descriptions
of what could come in this gateway.
Spirit can reveal cryptically now,
which you must interpret somehow.

Powerful energy is here to employ
to shine, grow, and thrive.
Be of service and align, buoy
to your highest possibilities to live.
Such actions could lead to the belief
humanity and Gaia could get some relief.

Allow more of your truth to shine through
though darkness, pain and suffering prevail,
explore the new, discard an old purview.
Despite our efforts hope might not unveil
the light we seek for positive change.
But we can try to re-arrange.

Not an easy possibility to do.
Many gurus and leaders have different ideas.
They proselytize their diverse view
using full range of the medias.
In this time of Eclipse Gateway transition,
let's hope we end up with guts and intuition.

Seeing 11:11

11:11 is a powerful awakening code that many spiritual seekers are frequently seeing...There are layers of meaning when it comes to seeing this number...like the Profound Archangelic Energy 11:11 carries...Or the deeper meaning and opportunity that is opened for you, when you see 11:11. Melanie Beckler

On clocks in cars, inside a dwelling–
anywhere 11:11 can appear,
listen to what the angels are telling.
At this time the angels are near.
> 1 stands for a pillar of light,
> an ascension column to enlight.

Anywhere 11:11 can appear,
even below digital timer on TV.
An angel might whisper in my ear,
(My, wouldn't it be heavenly?)
> unlocks deeper level of truth in soul
> and guidance how to perform our role.

Listen to what the angels are telling.
Four archangels are on call.
Four columns of light is compelling.
Perhaps can share best protocol?
> You're in the center: I Am in one.
> Mind-heart portal has begun.

At this time angels are near.
Get in synch and align.
Pathway of embodiment freer
from crystalline core to the divine.
> I AM pillar links heaven to earth,
> who we really are and path since birth.

One stands for a pillar of light—
can be circled by four for the four directions.
Diamond light to create, blessings, insight
as you shine your truth, make best selections.
> 11:11 is a symbol you are safe and supported
> by your angels as some have reported.

An Ascension Column to enlight
and elevate psychic abilities in you.
Soul-gifts radiate well-being, delight
to serve, dive into embodying what's true.
> I'm not sure I am properly connected
> to perform what 11:11 expected.

What is Going On?

Some people think everything that happens
is part of some cosmic plan. Every life
has a set time span, coding, free will.
When it is your time— you go?

Some people think events are random,
synchronicities and accidents just
part of the roll of the dice. No control
over what happens–equipment fails—you go?

Some people believe we are holograms.
Aliens tweaked our DNA. We are starseeds
brought here to repopulate after last extinction.
We are here until the next wipe-out, then we'll go?

Some people speculate we have a role
to play, all the world is a stage concept.
Scripts written before birth. We are to learn
our parts, act them out and then go?

How much control we have over events
and our choices is debatable. A divine
creator with earthly leaders help guide us,
have their own agenda for us, then we go?

Is their some digital systems which keeps
track of each life? Does an Akashic Record
store our life times? All an illusion? We
are dreaming? Watch a show, then go?

As I witness the violence, chaos, destruction
going on and I'm powerless to stop it, I wonder
why I am here? Who do I report this experience
to when it is time for me to go?

How many times and places have I gone?
Anywhere did I figure it out? In the vast cosmos
we must be just one experiment. Wonder if any
questions answered somewhere? Wherever I go?

I prefer certain climates in all its interpretations.
I'd like to shine light on some of them with certainty.
But darkness obscures my view, I must adapt to change.
Will I remain unknowing until I go?

Listening to My Life

Before I can tell my life what I want to do with it, I must listen to my life telling me who I am. Parker Palmer

What guidance am I listening to?
Where does it come from? A higher realm?
A counselor on this plane, a guru?
The prospect tends to overwhelm.
            How do I make a connection?
            What is the source of my introspection?

Where does it come from? A higher realm?
Angelic or alien? Subconscious through dream?
Just where is the source? Who's at the helm?
Must I listen to whomever shows up?
            How do I assess their intentions?
            Do I want to enact their conventions?

A counselor on this plane, a guru
proselytizing some slanted beliefs?
What do I need to breakthrough?
Advocating to follow archaic chiefs?
            How do I trust any paths—
            especially when I witness aftermaths.

The prospect tends to overwhelm.
How can I tell my life what to do?
Does my life intend to whelm
certain tendencies? What is true?
            I guess with life it is okay
            to proceed in your best way?

How to make a connection?
Interpret dreams? Attempt prayer?
Rely on accessible sources for selection?
How can I reach for a deeper layer?
            Some intuitives seem to have insight
            into the human drama and plight.

What is the source of my introspection?
Gut reaction? Inborn code?
Open to an angelic inspection?
My circuits tend to overload?
            Telling a stubborn Aries how to live?
            Will I ever find out what to take or give?

178

In Need of Archangels

I need an uplift, body and soul.
My guardian angel needs assistance.
In order for me to perform my role
I need an upgrade to my persistence.
          I plead for the world, not just me.
          Our dilemma requires some creativity.

My guardian angel needs assistance.
Does she listen? Does she care?
Is she facing some resistance?
Wants some cooperation? I am just not aware?
          In any case she does not seem effective.
          Do I dig deeper to be reflective?

In order for me to perform my role
and be more cosmically guided,
am I ever to become whole?
Remain too earthly-sided?
          Am I on the wrong path?
          Headed for some dark aftermath?

I need an upgrade to my persistence
to feel supported, brighten my light.
I'm running out of time and patience.
Will archangels intervene and enlight?
          It is harder daily to cope.
          The planet's on a slippery slope.

I plead for the world, not just for me.
I'm lured to the promise of a Fifth dimension,
a peaceful, sustainable place with liberty.
What is the cosmic plan's intention?
          Until I learn, I dwell in wonder,
          trying to decide what to ponder.

Our dilemma requires some creativity
Anything I can contribute?
In order to build a new reality,
so many assets to re-distribute.
          What is the protocol
          to unite us all?

Message from Archangel Jeremiel

Archangel Jeremiel is stepping forward now to support you in reflecting, and reviewing the choices, actions, and even challenges that have led you to where you are right now, and right here. Melanie Beckler*

With an unfamiliar name ending in el,
I could have guessed an angel or archangel.
But I never heard of Jeremiel.

No matter where it came from, the message
has some suggestions for folks of any age
who are reflecting and want to engage.

"Honor how far you've come.
Honor how much you've learned, the wisdom
you've gained, the readiness and openness..." to become.

"Cultivate your energy and cultivate openness now,
will empower you onward." You'll discover how.
"Turn the page on what has been and begin again." somehow.

"Stepping into uncharted territory with love
and joy in your heart". Give past a shove.
"Your future's highest possibilities" you're thinking of.

"Listen to the guidance of your heart and allow
whatever is happening to be okay." and follow.
"You have what it takes to fulfill soul mission." below.

"Don't get overwhelmed with all the details
of HOW to create the big picture." what it entails.
"Or overwhelm with list of things to do." derails.

"Trust in the process, listen to your inner guidance.
Claim the blessings available." take a chance.
"Integrate the lessons of your past" to enhance.

Embracing what is now with love and openness.
Knowing this empowers you in the present" none the less.
"Your highest Divine Timelime in synch with love at highest"?

Well, Jeremiel, you're a little elusive
with vague tactics and not conclusive.
I need love light to be less reclusive.

Responsibility

Apparently it is our responsibility
to raise our vibration and align
to our highest possibility—
part of the universal design.
>It is up to each of us to play our part
>with courage, conviction, compassion, heart?

To raise our vibration and align
is not easy in a heavy world.
We tend to wait for a sign
a New World has unfurled.
>How will we play our part for access
>to higher intentions for success?

To our highest possibility
have we been DNA encoded?
Will we gain accessibility
if we haven't downloaded?
>We are to spark light
>to help the world aright?

Part of the universal design
is our expanding and growing?
Can we choose to resign?
Will we remain unknowing?
>Are we really responsible
>for what is incomprehensible?

It is up to each of us to play our part?
What is our script? Who is designer?
Are we a wannabe earthling upstart?
Are we to become a cosmic maligner?
>If we are puppets, who controls strings?
>Are we holograms prey to what program brings?

With courage, conviction, compassion, heart—
are these efforts and ourselves enough
to create for Earth a sustainable restart?
Are we responsible star stuff?
>Will our legacy remain in the "cloud"?
>How much responsibility will be allowed?

My Vision

My eyes
are blurred by
cataracts and my tears.
Sometimes I see too much or not
enough.

My eyes
see foggy words.
A film covers vision.
I seem to dream clear-eyed and can
focus.

When I'm
awake, they blur
no matter occasion.
Will my vision clarify? See
mission?

March Forecast 2020

The darkest hours are here. You may recognize this in all the things you know or imagine, the plague, the pestilence, the climate, the politics. In countries near and far, there is chaos and darkness. There is fear and anger. There is suffering. Sara Wisemen

My 80th birthday is this March. Happy Birthday?
The channeling indicates we will feel
suffering, real desolation in the collective soul.

She claims separation is a myth and we are One
with all other sentient and non-sentient beings,
with everything that is Source. Not comforting.

We can never be separated from the universe.
Place this understanding in your heart?
I'm having enough trouble as an Earthling.

Add it is hard to believe what is shown.
Some of it is slanted and not correct.
Not very helpful for uplifting.

She suggests to find the truth by connecting
to the light within. Understand what is light
and what is love. Go into stillness and rest.

Don't allow mind to be in control. Let darkness
rage it will burn itself out soon. We are nearing
the end and relief is in sight. I need convincing.

The key is not to lose our minds. It is easy
to get confused, be easily swayed. Lead
from your soul, from a place of Oneness.

Let inner truth, the inner light be your guide.
The dawn is coming. The soul collective wakes up,
the old structures fight to maintain their power.

When light arrives it is impossible to hold dark.
We are to trust changes are happening. Trust
the universe supports you on your path.

As the collective soul moves through darkness,
it is very dark. Why do we need to experience
such darkness? Part of a cosmic dictator's plan?

For now, blaze light. Refrain from drama, keep
yourself from despair. Connect daily to light
within and without. Give light. Receive light.

All this seems airy-fairy in a heavy 3D duality
reality, currently having a really rough patch.
Hope and trust are hard to sustain us right now.

We never seem to maintain the light
and serve all humanity with peace,
justice, compassion and kindness.

I guess I will remain depressed by
the lack of light progress. I will be
seeking stars in the night.

Life is a Spiral

Our spiritual journey through life does not unfold in a straight line. It's not linear. Rather, our life path unfolds like a spiral, where you continually come back to things you thought you'd learned and understood...to uncover even deeper truths. Melanie Beckler

Apparently energy from the March Full moon on the 9th
        the spiral path reaches a turning point. An incredible
opportunity to improve your life and align with profound healing.

Everyone twists and turns together according to cosmic energy?
        At these turning points you can understand where you've
been, are now, and how to improve? A collective awakening?

Feels like Prometheus pushing the rock up a hill
        only to experience its downfall again. Go to the gym,
get more buff and try again? Awfully hard work.

Spirals can go up or down and I am not sure how
        much free will or leverage we have. Does our DNA
life chart overrun cosmic directives? Collective consciousness?

Are we trying to rise to the 5th dimension? Do we have enough
        collective cooperation to uplift our frequency?
Are we spiraling up or down? How much can we ever understand?

As I witness the division, inequities, violence–are we going down?
        Can we perform our life missions if connected to All
and our intentions can't lighten the heavy dark?

Obviously I have a way to go to comprehend this planet
        and my incarnation here and now. Gurus tend
to think humanity is heading in the right direction. I'm not sure.

April is Angel Month

Some proclaim April as Angel Month.
Hopefully every month is Angel Month,
but a worthy group to honor along with poetry.

Just eight days until April and the showers
have begun. Angel Month is the month more
love, hope and abundance arrives?

The earthly collective struggles with fear
and uncertainty about the coronavirus.
Humans shut-in and flowers bloom.

Numerologists want to help us connect
with angels, bring divine guidance and wisdom,
transmute fear to love, hope, happiness.

An epic Aries New Moon is coming up
so they want us to prepare for the divine
goodness ahead. Not sure I believe in all this.

But innately I do believe in angels. Bella,
my guardian angel may exist or not, but I
can imagine she does. I'll trust my gut.

In April I'll be 80 and ready for a cleansing,
letting go of the old for the new. I'll conjure
myself as Bella's cohort Rebella.

Miracles

All your worries and concerns are merely illusion. Sara Wiseman

The moment you turn your attention
to something real, like nature all your
worries go away?

The world was created for our joy?
We are meant to be awestruck?
I need a re-alignment for my assignment.

Yes, there is beauty, but destructive
forces of cosmos, Earth and humanity
are still hostile to survival.

When I see the pain and suffering
of all life forms, I tend to yearn
for a respite from my overwhelmed senses.

I do not know what is real or illusion.
Miracles do occur, but disasters seem
at least as prevalent.

There is no escaping our responsibilities
to steward inanimate and animate matter.
Is that the purpose we are here now?

If we are multi-dimensional and we spend
time in other realms, what illusions and conclusions
could we bring back to guide us?

Is reality a consensual guess? Miracles
part of the illusion that we actually impact
existence? Are we DNA coded how to go?

After all this time you would think humanity
could have evolved to get a better grip, accept
miracles, illusions and reality as life's journey.

Musing About the Afterlife

If our souls are eternal— entering
and exiting many forms–or none,
this earthly existence is one of many.

This is an experiment of bio-beings
in linear time in Earth's 3D experience.
Some think they are in 4D and even 5D.

Some believe this is all an illusion,
some computer game or hologram
and Earth is a misguided experiment.

Some of our cosmic kin may have
seeded us as a cosmic joke for their
entertainment–our suffering. Take resources.

How many games does the cosmos
create? Do we have to experience them
all and if we're eternal–eternally new ones?

If there are dimensions of various
frequencies we cannot discover except
in dreams (or nightmares) we're endlessly on call.

Webs and waves throughout the cosmos
to navigate infinitely. I was hoping for a break,
a vacation to regroup in a utopian place.

Are we forever sent out of a Garden of Eden,
trying fruitlessly, never forgiven and
always unknowing? No respite?

Humans are a strange lot, slow to change,
slower to steward the planet given. I am
ready to move on and hope for the best.

Future Climate

Here on Earth, we're exposed
to asteroids hitting the Earth,
eventual changes in the Sun,
changes in Earth's climate,
things we're doing to Earth's climate.
If we want to survive we need
to become a multi-planet species.
That's further down the road, but
the first wave is going to be explorers.
John M. Grunsfeld

After Us

What will those who come after us think of us? Will they envy us that we saw butterflies and mockingbirds, penguins and little brown bats? Derrick Jensen

Most likely they would be mad
at our morasses,
left what's bad.

They might want to leave as well.
Earth is a junkyard.
Left in Hell.

They might think we were batty.
Poor stewards of Earth:
Mad-Hatty.

We're planet killers
ill-willers.

Imagining

Imagine a better place
with peace, love, joy for
human race?

All of earthly creations
harmonious like
vacations.

No violence, sustainable,
treated with respect,
enable.

Though just fantasy,
dream to me.

The Starry Path

Two days before the new decade, I slogged
to exercise class in dim morning light.
Not much last night's sleep logged.
I saw three, tiny, shiny stars—bright.
      Such a positive omen.
      A good year's start for men and women?

To exercise class in dim morning light
I followed three golden, cut-out stars,
from the side of my car to front door I delight
in the one-inch parking lot grounded stars.
      Just these three stars from my car to door.
      I'd never seen such droppings before.

Not much last night's sleep logged,
I needed some zip and uplifts.
My mind felt heavy and fogged.
But with the stars, my mood shifts.
      Three stars left for me to see.
      Their origins a mystery.

I saw three, tiny, shiny, stars— bright,
flat on the dark pavement for me to spot.
My curiosity fueled in pale sunlight.
Wasn't this a positive sign? Why not?
      It isn't every day such a star appears,
      to illuminate, rouse cheers,

such a positive omen.
I wonder what it means for this upcoming decade?
Will I and others have the acumen
to come to the planet's aid?
      Stars appear to enlight?
      Will I decode the stars right?

A good year's start for men and women?
I will interpret the stars as encouragement,
sent by Earth or cosmic citizen
to assuage my discouragement?
      I welcome this starry path
      and ponder the aftermath.

A New Decade

A new
decade begins
2020. Nineteens
are over. Move forward with peace
and hope?

Global
urgent issues
must be addressed. Can we
act in time to thrive and also
survive?

Can we
change power and
leadership for common
good? We need connections to bring
less greed.

Perhaps
we need a change
in consciousness or a
species stewardship of Gaia—
exchange?

Earth will
recover without
us. So perhaps we will
choose to die off so the Earth can
reseed.

The Earth
will prevail but will
humanity? We are
at a crossroads. I choose saving
the Earth.

Letting Go to Free

All the gurus and numerologists–
predictors of all persuasions
tend to be apologists—
discard Old World preoccupations
  to let go and open a New World view
  to let go what no longer serves you.

Predictors of all persuasions
indicate the planet is changing
all living situations,
world-views exchanging.
  Some are hopeful our attention
  will be for an uplifting intention.

Tend to be apologists
for our fateful turns.
Blaming or denying these twists
which makes Gaia flood and burn.
  We seem to have forgotten our earthly mission—
  somehow lost in transmission?

Discard Old World preoccupations.
Time to act in sustainable ways.
Old World Order tumbles, new occasions
to refresh, renew, re-invent replays.
  Inequity, disharmony, division.
  New World to envision.

To let go and open a New World view
means becoming aware and act.
Find out what you can do
to enlighten and how best to react.
  Bring darkness into the light.
  End sadness for delight.

To let go what no longer serves you
can mean relationships end, beliefs freed.
Changes in jobs, locations, point of view,
to create a sustainable, caring need.
  Let go what weighs you down.
  See how many ways you've grown.

What Are We Made of?

Are
we
creatures
of love or
hate, lukewarm Earthlings
struggling to make our way, stewards?

Are
we
ready
to take on
changes of climates
to perhaps maintain survival?

I
look
around
and see some
pathetic people.
Are we up to uplifting Earth?

I
am
not that
positive
or optimistic.
Perhaps waste and greed buries us.

If
we
can't' shift
and uplift
Earth gets some better
stewards? We vacate scene? Die out?

Please Donate

Donate
to every
good cause would bankrupt me.
Daily solicitations to
support.

It seems
requests needed
globally for diverse
causes. But how do we know if they're
legit?

On-line
web sites, info
available but are
they reliable? Money go
to need?

Lots to
repair, heal, find
solutions for our well-
being- all life on this plundered
planet.

Why go
to space? Escape our
responsibility
to justice and equity here
on Earth?

We must
decide
our priorities for
resources diminish, as we
muddle.

I would
like to be an
optimist when I see
glimmers of hope, but really not
enough?

Endurance

Maybe
if we knew why
negative things happen
we could endure the suffering
better?

Maybe
if we knew the
reason it happens we
could cope or understand, accept
just why?

Maybe
our ignorance
keeps it repeating and
we are overwhelmed and can not
stop it.

Maybe
our love, caring
brings us more than we can
bear, our knees buckle and our heart
explodes.

Endure
for what? For why?
What is necessary to
experience? Can't we do
better?

What do
we bring ourselves
to the conundrum of
earthly awareness, hoping for
progress?

En-Masse

From mountaintops to crevasses
gather the masses,
the lads and the lasses
from all different classes
put on clear-eyed glasses.
Try looking-glasses.

Confront the jackasses
creating morasses.
They taint our repasses
burn forests and grasses
pollute water and air with gases
mine land for metals like brasses.
There are no free passes.

Time to unclass.
Outclass.
Take on the brass.
Alas
amass
before hour-glass
of climate change surpasses.
Kick their asses.

Got Your Number?

Numerologists and astrologers play
with numbers to prophesize
our destinies in a numerous way.
To play with numbers is wise?
      My life determined by birth date?
      The cosmos and I always relate?

With numbers to prophesize
2-22 should unleash cosmic dose
of love and abundance, emphasize
love is ruling force, keep compassion close.
      Practice self trust.
      For creativity–a must.

Our destinies in a numerous way
requires some calculation
for possibilities to array
for connecting and collaboration.
      I never was fond of math
      or computing on my path.

To play with numbers is wise?
Some feel computations guide
them and they surmise,
numbers are on their side.
      Not being a great calculator
      I'm not the best evaluator.

My life determined by birth date?
Did I pre-select time and place?
Does free will at all dictate fate?
Did my life chart erase?
      Did I come in with a clean slate?
      Decide when I will graduate?

The cosmos and I always relate?
Consciousness and form part of cosmic plan
no matter where I incarnate?
Left to do what I can?
      Live by the numbers? I hope not fully.
      No mathematician is yours truly.

A Choppy Time

A choppy time for the planet. We have passed through some energetic openings recently allowing more energy and light into our collective reality. The planet will quite likely remain in choppy waters for some time to come. Steve Ahnael Nobel

There is much fear and confusion
in the collective... deliberately stirred
by hidden lower forces–the conclusion?
Our current vision appears blurred.
       With all the changes we face,
       we need guides for the human race.

In the collective...deliberately stirred
by dark forces leading to addictions.
People's heart-breaking journey spurred
by drug, alcohol, entity possession afflictions.
       Apparently each soul has its own journey.
       Making light choices is a key.

By hidden lower forces–the conclusion?
Where do they come from. Do we have free will?
We can raise our frequency, pray for an infusion
of guidance and support? Angels fit the bill?
       Some people pause, abort, fall into darkness.
       Some choose a tour through soul starkness.

Our current vision appears blurred.
Powerful divisions and emotions sway
so love and compassion aren't transferred.
How long will this choppy time stay?
       In order for some to cope,
       they try denial or hope.

With all the darkness we face
can we persist and resist, take charge?
Much of civilization has fallen from grace.
I get pretty pessimistic, by and large.
       We have to start with our highest intention.
       But there are dark leaders I won't mention.

We need guides for the human race—
cosmic, earthling, supernatural?
Will a fifth dimension ever take place?
What can we work on that is actual?
       Can we calm and repair these choppy times?
       It effects all life forms, matter and climes.

If We Are to Stay

If
we
are all
together
in this global mess,
what will we do about it? Not?

If
we
cannot
agree what
to do, can we win?
What is enough to do to stay?

If
we
are not
allowed to
try to steward, then
what will the planet do to us?

If
we
fumble
the planet,
where would we go and
where would we be welcomed to stay?

Addressing Now

When you look for your answer in the future, you miss the wisdom of Now.
Sara Wiseman

If there is always the next Mystery
with the same insatiable desire
to know what's ahead, as she says,
yet Now contains all the answers,
will I get stuck and never figure it out?

She suggests if you don't like your Now
ask what it is teaching you? Who do
you call when efforts stall and you
can't comprehend All? If we are here
to learn and serve the light...How?

Even if I get answers and understand
why we are in the predicament we are in,
that does not mean I have the opportunity
to change them? What am I meant to do
about all the challenges facing the planet?

I never was very good at puzzles, patiently
placing the pieces to create the full picture.
Are we coded in our DNA? Following a life
chart? Do we have free will to tweak our
destiny? Just performers following scripts?

Who are the playwrights? Who creates
the life charts and codes the DNA? Now
is but a blip which will dissolve before
we know why we came to this planet
at this time? Now is key to future? Hmm.

Outside the Window

Outside
the window, spring
lushes green amid bright
splashes of flowering plants, right
on time.

Inside
I do yoga
sitting on a chair, gaze
through the glass. Openings are
shut down.

Daily
we are urged to
shelter in place, social
distance, while nature is blooming
outward.

Wind swirls
branches, my limbs
controlled by patterns, my
heart wants freedom of movement, dance
wildly.

Planted
as the trees and
flowers, I wait to grow
expand, explore and can pick path
myself.

Body
hunkers down, but
my mind creates it's own
reality and dreams a new world
for all.

Until the End of Time

In the fullness of time all that lives will die... As our trek across time will make clear, life is likely transient, and all understanding that arose with its emergence will most certainly dissolve with its conclusion. Nothing is permanent. Nothing is absolute. Brian Greene

Many theories propose our origins, life's meaning.
Pick a theory you want to believe in or remain in doubt.
Life and thought might be a minute oasis in comic gleaning.
Changes in understanding will still come about.
> A dark future bereft of stars?
> Gulped in black hole, collision scars?

Pick a theory you want to believe in or remain in doubt.
The universe is expanding, does it ever end?
Remain open to what still will sprout?
Is the cosmos our foe, indifferent, a friend?
> Future dictated by inflation?
> Still room for Einstein equation?

Life and thought might be a minute oasis in cosmic gleaning.
Will "cloud" or Akashic Records record our existence?
Will Earth desist its burgeoning greening?
Any worth to humanity's persistence?
> Are we charged by our DNA
> to become what we are today?

Changes in understanding will still come about.
Can our imagination navigate the unknown?
Can physics explain how a mind figures things out?
Can old beliefs be overthrown?
> Can consciousness be demystified?
> Will our quest be unsatisfied?

A dark future bereft of stars?
Rejoice that we still have light?
Are we perpetual avatars?
Will black hole slurp be our plight?
> Future requires more energy? Starkness.
> Are we "brief crack of light" between eternities of darkness?

Gulped in black hole, collision scars?
We can reach for eternity, but not touch it?
Debate continues in theories' wars.
Natural selection? Or entropic—two step vouch it?
> Will entropy end universe's evolution?
> You can pick your own resolution.

Plea to Dark Entities

Please leave
me alone. Don't
leave dark cords and threads for
my masseuse to pull out to then
free me.

I need
my light to shine
fully, not strangled or
entangled in darkness, to heal
and serve.

Darkness
duels with light, takes
hope for a lighter world.
Daylight to act, night to rest? Need
darkness?

I pray
light will prevail.
Let us all envision.
The universe is dark and vast–
return?

Leave
Earth alone, free
to enlight, sparkle from
dark negative duality
to shine?

When I Cross Over

When I cross over I do not know
what to expect and to where.
I'm in perhaps my last decade now.
Perhaps it's time to prepare?
How do you prepare for the unknown?
How much of my life will I own?

What to expect and to where
is a big question.
Any clues to become aware
of any possible suggestion?
Will there be some divine intervention?
Is that some hopeful invention?

I'm in perhaps my last decade now.
If I'm to get it done, I must not dawdle.
I must create my final show,
dance despite my waddle.
Make priorities what to do?
Enough time to follow through?

Perhaps it's time to prepare
to assist Gaia's sustainable future
and make people more aware.
We have a planet to nurture.
What I do is more than about me.
I must be concerned with acts of humanity.

How do you prepare for the unknown?
How much responsibility do I have
to embrace or to disown?
I get confused how to behave.
Days I'd like to just cocoon,
too tired to enhance or prune.

How much of my life will I own?
Admit mistakes, ask forgiveness?
I admit to being otherworldly prone.
I fantasize to bring more happiness.
I go forward with curiosity,
grounded for reciprocity?

Cosmic Climate

I think that an advanced civilization
will modify their own planets
to be more stable, to prevent asteroid impacts
and dangerous climate fluctuations.

Daivd Grinspoon

Valentines for Gaia

Roses are red, Violets are blue. Please go green. The world needs you.
A Mutts Valentine

Your roses are red.
Your violets are blue.
I'll try to go green
because I love you.

Now red is for blood.
Blue is for flood.
Gray is pollution.
We need green solution.

We have work to clear
up your atmosphere,
to change darkness to shine–
beloved planet of mine.

Our Future

Any
prophesies right
or despite warnings, we
made the wrong choices and just
happened?

Any
force dominant?
Out of balance to save
the planet and all the living
beings?

Any
hope to control
and unite all the parts
a gathering together like
Isis?

Maybe
cosmos predicts
our evolution and
Earth's experiment's ending
not us?

Transhumanists

Our next
step in our slow
evolution maybe
as bio-being to merge with a
robot.

Hybrids
could gain their own
consciousness and explore
space better than just flesh and blood
humans.

Brains get
connected to
computers and the "Cloud".
We could probe space anywhere, but
person?

They may
replicate and
procreate themselves to
populate the cosmos. People
stay home.

Were we
seeded from some
alien race? At stage to
join in seeding new A.I. for
space race?

As the
scientists play,
bio-beings have a task
to steward Earth. Nowhere else to
go —yet.

Becoming or Evolving

Are we
becoming or
evolving for the best
or in time to improve, preserve,
ourselves?

Or do
we become an
individual, who
contributes and serves best for the
planet?

If we
evolve it seems
we develop slowly.
So many years just refining our
bodies.

If we
become are we
tweaking our brains to
think, create, invent and discover
better?

What is
highest choice for
planet and us to speed
up our equipment to save us?
Have time?

Pallas

Pallas
the most cratered
asteroid in the whole
asteroid belt is like battered
golf ball.

We might
find more abused
asteroids as we find
more asteroids picked on by the
cosmos.

We were
bombarded too.
We could be again, then
what happens to Earth could be like
Pallas?

The Pale Blue Dot

> *Look again at that dot. That's here. That's home. That's us. On it everyone you know, everyone you ever heard of, every human being who ever was, lived out their lives, the aggregate of our joy and suffering, thousands of confident religions, ideologies and economic doctrines, every hunter and gatherer, every hero and coward, every creator and destroyer of civilizations, every king and peasant, every young couple, every mother and father, hopeful child, inventor and explorer every teacher of morals, every corrupt politician, every "superstar", every "supreme leader", every saint and sinner in the history of our species lived here–on a mote of dust suspended in a sunbeam.* Carl Sagan

Voyager 1 spacecraft took the photo
just past Saturn's orbit of Earth as
a bright speck within a sunbeam.

Our pale blue dot in an infinite universe
is indeed on a minuscule scale, but
to us it is our beloved blue marble.

We need to figure out our part in
the cosmic conundrum, learn to be
better stewards. Listen to Carl Sagan.

Scientists are not sure if we are but
an itty-bitty ort on a flat plate or in a bubble
and curved to curl back into itself.

Whatever the theories, we are expanding
to the Big Chill, but currently they do not
think there will be a Big Crunch.

Our pale blue dot gets bashed by meteorites
and mashed by people's technology, mining
and waste. Gaia has been plundered.

So while we can, we can experience our dot
as a period at the end of a sentence or a lens
on the mysteries of all life here and the multiverse.

Arrokoth: The Snowman- Shaped Space Object

Arrokoth is a pristine, primordial cosmic body—
the farthest, most primitive object in the solar system
to be visited by our spacecraft. A photo op.

Few craters impact its surface, no water,
Its also entirely ultrared, or highly reflective,
commonplace in Twilight Zone or Kuiper Belt.

To the human eye Arrokoth would look
dark brown like molasses. Reddish color
indicates organic molecules.

Frozen methane but no water found.
Arrokoth is 22 miles long tip to tip,
a roly-poly snowman.

No rings or satellites indicate it is
4.5 million years old–back to the
formation of the solar system.

Perhaps they were an orbiting pair
that melded, causing a fused body
called a contact binary from nebula clouds.

Arrokoth means sky in the language
of North American Powhatan people.
Emerging technology will take us around Pluto.

We will go deeper into the Kuiper Belt
to find other dwarf planets and objects,
to study geological and geophysical details.

Poor Arrokoth probably will not be highly
sought after because of other potentially
richer resources to exploit elsewhere.

Lucky Arrokoth still has time to itself.
Look, but don't touch approach? People
are a very touchy-feeling bunch. Beware.

Searching for Exoplanets

Whenever a space object is discovered,
my fascination, wonder, excitement increases.
Planets, a fraction the mass of a star uncovered,
found by what the planet releases,
 detected by radial velocity, microlensing, astrometry
 direct imaging, moonlight and transit photometry

My fascination, wonder, excitement increases.
Intelligent life could exist there, but not welcome us.
Some of earthly belief and theory ceases.
For what purpose are we making this fuss?
 Curiosity or exploitation?
 Looking for human relocation?

Planets a fraction the mass of a star uncovered
at an astonishing rate with the hope for complex life?
How much of the big picture have we covered?
We have been ingenious, but difficulties are rife.
 Exoplanets often found near the stars in orbit.
 Scientists study stars to find an exo-planet.

Found by what the planet releases,
by methods developed to detect shifts—
a wobble, find distance, dimming decreases.
With every discovery our knowledge uplifts.
 I shutter at the complexity of math,
 but thrill at findings' aftermath.

Detected by radial velocity, microlensing, astrometry—
exoplanets, just pinpoints of light, are found.
Part of the cosmic sacred geometry?
The impact on us is profound.
 Our future possibilities expand,
 as we come to understand.

Direct imagery, moonlight, transit photometry
enhance our access to these small dark objects.
All is very technically challenging for me.
I remain a star-gazing, earthbound subject.
 Space continues to amaze me,
 leads me into a maze creatively.

Habitable Exo-planets

Recently scientists found K2-18B
124 light years away, twice the size
of Earth. They debate if it hosts life.

Currently called a Mini-Neptune
rather than Super-Earth. Scientists
still waffling with that definition.

It is within a habitable zone.
Hydrogen in atmosphere, then
watery layer, rocky iron core?

Many questions remain if it is
habitable for life to survive. Perhaps
water pressure too much for life.

Observing the cosmos with better
equipment reveals exo-planets
of great diversity and promise.

We are spaced out on universe,
searching for life–and escape route
from earthly extinction.

Extinctions by meteorite strikes,
planetary collision, gamma rays,
solar flares, eruptions, snowball conditions.

To preserve humanity, can we only survive
if we make a planetary move? Mars or exoplanets
our only hope? Advanced beings will move in?

Space Surprises

Marsquakes,
the biggest space
explosion ever seen,
now new mini-moon orbiting
for Earth?

Object
caught in Earth's
orbit three years ago—
named 2020CD3—
surprise!

Its small.
They think it's here
temporarily, but
maybe it will stay as mini
new moon?

Maybe
it is not moon,
but a space craft checking
us out, deciding whether to
approach?

Here to
save us from our
eminent extinction?
Or maybe beating us humans
to it?

We will
have to wait and
see what happens. Aiming
a meteorite or comet
at us?

Space is
vast, full of new
discoveries and some
surprises, can't predict cosmic
unknowns.

The Biggest Explosion

The biggest explosion astronomers
have found is in Ophiuchus Supercluister
in Ophiuchus Constellation.

This explosion left a dent in space.
300 million light-years away,
it was created by a black hole

Black holes don't just gobble up
material, but spit it out in jets
or beams. A biggest burp?

15 Milky Way galaxies in a row
would fit into the crater this explosion
punched into the clusters of hot gas.

Clusters of galaxies are the largest
known structures in the universe.
Gravity holds thousands of galaxies together.

This explosion is five times greater
than MS0735 + 74 which was the previous
largest and most powerful explosion.

Who knows what will come next?
The cosmic mysteries expand with
the cosmos, so much unknown.

I'm just glad it was far way
and a black hole did not gobble
us up to vomit into vast darkness.

Otherworldly Experiences

Reports of near death encounters
reveal a globally similar tunnel of light
leading to a paradisiacal place.
They are given a choice to return or not.

Damage to head sometimes brings
unexpected talents. Is thought creation
in the brain or is mind a transmitter
of consciousness, originating somewhere?

Psychics and various intuitives can see
beyond time and into other dimensions.
How many illusions do we experience
as we try to decipher if anything is real?

Are we holograms, pawns in a computer
game, recorded in Akashic Records or "Cloud".
How do we choose what to believe and do?
Are we encoded before birth? Soul codes?

Many people from different backgrounds
believe in Other Worlds and various creation
theories. Do any paths lead to our highest good?
Our creativity spawns more choices. Free will?

My curiosity inhabits many worlds since childhood.
Dreams are another dimension of our
multi-dimensional being? When Earth gets heavy,
lighten up in another realm? Otherworldly visitations?

Some claim aliens are already among us
or hover in the sky. Are we shifting to 5D?
Who will take over wounded Earth when
we go extinct? Is humanity up for the job?

Other Worlds are a source of hope and fear.
It is not clear what is to come or what exists
beyond time. Other Worldly transfers may not
alleviate our responsibilities as stewards of Gaia.

Recycling the Cosmos
Everything ends and begins, closes and opens, dies and is born. Sara Wisemen

If everything ends and begins,
    it seems kind of wasteful. If things end
        is the new beginning assured?

With reincarnation does a soul ever die?
    Does it just shift containers and dimensions?
        Human lives end to give births space to grow?

Earth is like Shiva who destroys and renews.
    The cosmos explodes, reorganizes matter.
        So much energy into creating chaos.

Nature replenishes, but as we destroy habitat
    will the climate conditions allow regrowth?
        Many extinct species do not return.

Endings bring sadness and fear.
    Beginnings bring new expressions and hope.
        Too much violence, light/dark struggle.

We are to trust the cosmos knows what it's doing
    and we are part of some multiversal plan?
        Does each experiment get timed out?

When Earth is wiped out or a planetary collision
    scatters debris into the universe, does "cloud" remain?
        Some things lost in oblivion?

The only constant is change. Consciousness transferrable?
    Could the cosmos settle down to more peaceful goals?
        Will the unknowable remain unknown always?

Why did the dinosaurs have to die and leave humans in charge?
    As we plasticize the planet, will we make Gaia unsustainable?
        Do endings mean progress with new beginnings?

UFOs

So many witness UFOs
experts can't explain.
Guess who knows?

Globally governments hide
reports of sightings.
Facts collide.

Some see aliens beings.
Cover-ups of what
they're seeing.

We are not alone,
undertone.

Realizations

No matter what I try
to learn and comprehend,
I am left with too many "Why"?
Is the cosmos really our friend?
        They say we are never alone.
        Why am I not commitment prone?

To learn and comprehend
seems to be an earthly goal.
But I cannot pretend
to understand parts of the whole:
        the duality of dark and light,
        the struggle to set things aright.

I am left with too many "Why?
Why the violence, abuse and pain?
Why the need for a global outcry?
Why do issues return again and again?
        Why the conflict, urge to win
        only to lose to our chagrin?

Is the cosmos really our friend
as it expands in darkness, sprinkles
light amid explosions which don't end?
Amid bubbles, disc, waves, wrinkles?
        Some seek salvation with the Divine,
        unknowable, unable to define.

They say we are never alone
in the universe or when we incarnate.
Angels, life charts, help us postpone,
choose wisely where to participate?
        Are we form-changers, live in multiple dimensions?
        Experience many milieu with different intentions?

Why am I not commitment prone
to Old World Order, many ground rules.
I witness and often groan
at the actions of negative leaders and fools.
        As fleshy creatures, Earth's our place.
        We'll need many adaptations to live in space.

Rules of Karma

Your head will tell you a million things about how things should or shouldn't be.
Give your head a rest, and follow the rules of karma. Sara Wiseman

Choose as wisely as you can, but also know
there are no mistakes, just soul lessons?
     When something is completed it will go away.
     When something is changing it will change.
     When something is real, it will remain.
The rules of karma are in effect at all times.

There are no mistakes, just soul lessons?
I guess that is a judgement call?
Somehow my confidence lessens.
Will we find a global protocol?
     What does the soul want to know this life?
     Does the soul have to learn in all this strife?

When something is completed it will go away?
Is this in our life code when we will die?
What obstacles are put in our way?
How much do we try? Why?
     Whatever we create goes into a "Cloud"?
     Can't certain things stay? Just await a shroud?

When something is changing it will change?
We have no free will? Just go with the flow?
Pandemics and climate cause us to rearrange.
We are afraid, suffering, don't know where to go.
     Change can renew and demolish the old,
     bring new ideas, opportunities, I'm told.

When something is real it will remain?
What was once real, will decay.
Are we illusions, tricks of our brain?
Multidimensional? Real in cosmic way?
     What is fantasy can be uplifting.
     Are we dimensionally shifting?

The rules of karma are in effect at all times.
How many sets of rules are we to abide by?
Any adjustments for different climes?
How many choices for us to provide by?
     Diversity remains and divides.
     We need help from better guides.

Cosmic Codes

Are we guided by cosmic codes?
Earth rules imbedded in our DNA?
Do we receive cosmic downloads?
Is it free will all the way?
      If our slate is cleared at birth,
      what is the purpose of life on Earth?

Earth rules imbedded in our DNA?
Must we reincarnate when we forget
our progress in past lives? Nothing will stay
in our consciousness–maybe "cloud", Internet?
      Before all the high tech to record,
      how do we know if we're on board?

Do we receive cosmic downloads
with dreams, intuition and visions?
What if our equipment implodes?
Are we able to make revisions?
      What essence devised a cosmic plan?
      Certainly not a befuddled human.

Is it free will all the way?
How do we conjure images and thought?
What influences hold sway?
Are all our efforts just for naught?
      How does our will know it is free?
      Just what is free will meant to be?

If our slate is cleared by birth
why make it so we try to muddle through?
What is such guidance worth?
It seems a cruel thing to do.
      Humanity has had a long time to learn.
      Times up? Some other beings' turn?

What is the purpose of life on Earth?
To follow? To lead? To create?
Any insights for us to unearth?
What is the best way to participate?
      I am in no way amused
      by the knowledge I'm refused.

Wisdom of Uncertainty

In detachment lies the wisdom of uncertainty, in the wisdom of uncertainty lies the freedom from our past, from the known. And in our willingness to step into the unknown, the field of our possibilities, we surrender ourselves to the creative mind that orchestrates the dance of the universe. This means that the search for security and certainty is actually an attachment to the known. And what is known? The known is our past. The known is nothing other than the prison of past conditioning. There is no evolution in that—absolutely none at all. And when there is no evolution, there is stagnation, entropy, disorder and decay. Uncertainty, on the other hand is the fertile ground of pure creativity and freedom. Derek Hough

Since I dwell in a state of unknowing,
I must be a wise woman indeed.
My lack of commitment is showing
gaps and what I need.
      I want to dance with the universe,
      to create and play with verse.

I must be a wise woman indeed
as I resist and persist against hierarchy.
For justice and compassion I plead,
try to sift out cultural malarkey.
      I have commitment issues to weigh
      as I blunder on my way.

My lack of commitment is showing
when I refuse to align with a cause
that's outdated and progress slowing.
I see suffering which make me question laws,
      Earth's 3D, duality solutions.
      makes me ponder planet's evolutions.

Gaps and what I need
can go unheeded, undetected.
Victims of human greed
leave some paths unselected.
      Inequity of opportunity and access
      has hindered humanity's success.

I want to dance with the universe
as a multidimensional, cosmic citizen.
I don't mind being obstinate, perverse
if I am an unwilling partisan.
      I don't have a firm grip on anything.
      I'm a wannabe bird with a limp wing.

To create and play with verse
has been my greatest gift and pleasure.
I seek the new and the diverse.
Creativity is my best treasure.
      I sift through detritus and hope,
      uncertain I can cope.

Climate of Uncertainty

First, how do we give everyone
a fair shot at opportunity and security in this new
economy? Second, how do we make technology
work for us and not against us–especially when it
comes to solving urgent challenges like climate change.
Third, how do we keep America safe and lead the
world without becoming its policeman?

Barak Obama

Wintery Spring

In the midst of winter, I found within me, an invincible summer. And that
makes me happy. For it says that no matter how hard the world pushes against
me, there's something stronger – something better, pushing right back.
Camus quote from The Plague sent by Kathy Ross

This morning as the rain returned, after
sunny, greening, springing days, Oregon
joined the shut-down, shelter in place order.

Only essential businesses are to remain open.
Parks are closed. Art and sport venues closed.
Health, delivery, grocery, take-out food workers–stay.

I listen to the rain splatter on the skylight,
watch rain drip from my backyard chi chair,
I know rain is essential so I'll adjust.

My plan to sit outside foiled. I delay dressing
until after lunch. Another rescheduled day
in self-quarantine. Screens and newspapers inform.

The Olympics in Japan postponed. Italy shows
some sign of improving. New hot spots emerge.
In the neighboring county— a viral death.

We are a few days past the spring equinox.
This winter of our discontent has a long way
to pass through spring for the hope of summer.

In the kindness and courage of others, I see
the brighter side of this pandemic, we connect
and touch in new ways. Pollution lessens.

But global leadership needs to address the suffering
from all perspectives. Trump should not appoint
a trophy hunter advocate to protect our environment.

Spring break means close more beaches so
partiers do not infect others when they return home.
We learn we are all in this together–at least some do.

As we contemplate new ways of thinking and acting,
perhaps an inner spark of light will guide our way
for a new dawn after a still star-strung night.

When the Sun Don't Shine

A gray pall hovers over the backyard.
Light rain splatters the window, three
streams of water overflow from the gutter.

A wind twirls the pinwheel, but not enough
gusto to tingle the wind-chimes, or provoke
the dandelion puffball brigade to reseed.

A bird on the power line chirps as another
bird flies by. The bird, beam gymnast or
trapeze artist, walks the wire with flare.

When the gutter gushes streams over
the backdoor and outdoor light, I tell
my husband who is not pleased to know it.

Through the back fence after days of absence
the orangish light returns to sparkle through the
slats. Same spot. Did neighbors shorten a timer?

My husband hustles to the mini-waterfalls,
gutter trowel in hand, hauling a ladder. He scoops
the goop. Mucky wet leaves fling to the ground.

I watch mentally balancing the ladder. He was
glad to cleanup the mess. I must admit I liked
the drip. I observe a mostly motionless scene.

Rain-shine does not lure me to my chi chair
like sunshine does. Behind the glass, I cuddle
in my red cape, social distancing, staying in.

My metal chi chair chills without me. I deep
breathe to balance my chakras. Looping chi,
cosmos to earth core, faces many barriers.

Contact in this viral, hand-washing, non-touching
world forces more introspection, a chance
to clean up our act and unfurl positive change.

Hope is a Sunny Day

It should rain tomorrow, so today
I am eager to gather some rays
and fiddle with chakras and chi.

In these uncertain times when movement
and commerce are curtailed, pollution
is diminishing and creativity increases.

Vacations become staycations as
people find ways to sustain and entertain
themselves, reach out without touching.

New ways to handle economics and
worker compensation, people caring
for each other, dealing as challenges arise.

Our grandson recovers rapidly, but faces
uncertainty when he can return to work
if any paychecks are coming, when isolation ends.

A friend falls and breaks her arm bringing
food to a shut-in neighbor. Calls and emails
keep track of each other and offer support.

So as I sit outside this sunny spring day,
despite uncertainty, I feel a sense of hope.
When the rains come, I will view them as cleansing.

Gearing Up

During a rain respite, benign drops spitting
at us, my husband hauls a ladder
to a hazelnut limb to re-hook Airlika.

The rusty angel was dangling upside
down by her feet, wind-dancing over
my chi chair. Now she toots her horn flying.

I foray in full protective gear into the backyard.
Shoes on for the first time in days. Thick, white
fleecy jacket and hood. Red Cape shawled.

It is overcast and sixty, but I look like
a bloody wooly mammoth about to
embark into the Arctic.

I carry my blue pillow to cover the wet chair
seat, the arms polka-dotted with rain.
Airlika, looks straight West above me.

A dandelion social distances beside me.
Others also appear to spread out. A plump
puffball shivers in gusts about the fill the gaps.

One tiny dandelion seed lands on my red cape.
I flick it to the ground. I do my deep breathes,
try to loop chi, razzle-dazzle my chakras.

Shadows sprint across the lawn at a hint
of sun. Bird-shadows speckle sky. Raindrops
sparkle in the grass until it clouds over again.

Wind-gusto spins the pinwheels and clangs
the wind-chimes. Tootsie, the weathervane angel
remains unmoved, refuses to budge.

A few bugs. For a while we seem in the birds'
flight pattern. Four in succession land on the power
pole, several balance on the power line.

Two birds, probably jays, exchanged spots.
One on power line flies down as another flies
up from the rhododendron.

I decide to go inside when the shadows
fade, don't shade. I watch three small birds
in the hazelnut branches, flitting about.

My husband comes out to check on me as it
has been over an hour. We study hazelnut
birds and pronounce them sparrows, tentatively.

We go inside. I shed my protective gear,
layer by layer. I kick off my shoes again,
wriggle my toes, thaw under my red cape.

Sitting outside and inside of our fifth acre
is all the 3D reality I see. News is pressed
onto pages and screens, as we flatten the curve.

Everyone I know is quarantined- several sick.
One with COVID-19. We do not know when our
vistas will expand. I'm gearing up for a long haul.

With a Heavy Heart

Thankfully Buddhist practice offers some helpful guidelines for how we can cultivate clear seeing and be with ourselves and others as we sit with the specter of climate change, or any more recent concerns such as the COVID-19 pandemic we currently face. Heather Krimsly

On this International Forest Day,
I head into the backyard in solidarity
with the trees and efforts to save the planet.

In the midst of the coronavirus pandemic, I am
sad to learn a dear friend is battling cancer.
My grandson sent home from work with fever.

Such a heavy heart. I'm on the verge of tears.
The sun tries hard to warm me. Budding plants
and trees try to uplift my spirit.

The grim-reaper of grass scythed the lawn
with a hand-mower and clipped the heads
off several dandelions. Not a mood booster.

A jay, as blue as the cloudless sky, hops
under the rhododendron, then beak full
flutters in the branches before chomping's done.

To the West, neighbors' laughing carries over
clear air. Sounds like several people. Hope
they are social distancing and partying legally.

To the East my neighbor, coughing juicily, walks
into his yard to mow. He greets a neighbor over
a mutual fence and asks if they are 6 feet apart.

The response is he will not tell Trump if they
aren't. Soon the power motor drones, mutes
voices. Annoyed, I decide to go inside.

There are emails of a friend's viral test result,
delayed, my cousin's nightmare trying to get
home from a Bahamas vacation cut short.

So I return to the Buddhist article guidelines
suggesting resting in the Unknown. Meditation
can help avoid vagaries of the mind, quick conclusions,

No blame. Do not judge for it creates disconnection,
and pulls the focus away from the issue into drama.
Return to a place of observing, respond skillfully.

Interdependence. We are intertwined with each
other no matter what concern we are addressing.
Our survival depends on understanding this fact.

Humans get distracted and tend to look away.
Dig deep into our own lives. We need to maintain
compassion for ourselves and others, defuse layers.

She suggests it is time for us all to wake up.
I am carrying a heavy heart. I'd like to lighten
the load, but still in quandary how to do so.

Seeing clearly is a prerequisite for effective action.
My cataract surgery in second eye is postponed.
My vision could be blurry for quite a while.

Blame for Hosting Coronavirus
World Pangolin Day is February 15th

Endangered pangolin for
cornonavirus?
Evens score?

Rare animals eaten and
medicines— in great
demand.

Once numerous now plundered,
host to a virus?
Blundered?

Animals for host?
Which liked most?

Unscheduled Days

I was never a fan of strict schedules,
few repetitive routines, not prone to boredom.
Creativity commands breaking rules.
Uncertainty breeds wisdom?
>Homebound due to coronavirus.
>Pandemic leads to fears of crisis.

Few repetitive routines, not prone to boredom—
I don't have trouble filling my time.
Remaining inside is not burdensome.
A dreamer, my creative goals are prime.
>Imagination is the spark
>to ignite light in the dark.

Creativity commands breaking rules
to get rid of the old and discover the new.
I tussle with 3D duality duels.
I'm exhilarated by what comes through.
>When I am at home alone
>I contact others by email and phone.

Uncertainty breeds wisdom?
Maybe so, but the global crisis needs cures.
Time for some risks, be venturesome?
Wait for breakthroughs that reassures?
>We require world-wide cooperation
>to meet the needs of every nation.

A dreamer, my creative goals are prime
to setting my daily schedule to include
time for contemplating ideas earthly and sublime.
I want to remain open, let optimism intrude.
>Also mundane chores, responsible choices,
>service to light, listening to diverse voices.

Imagination is the spark
to brighten and enlighten my day.
Take time to muse, amuse, defuse
challenges still in my way.
>Each day the schedule rearranges
>to take into account unexpected changes.

Vernal Equinox

This Spring Equinox is the earliest in many years.
Even the plants seem to be in a rush to bloom, as
we self-quarantine and learn we are all in this together.

No boundaries as the virus spreads. Everyone
could be infected. Some pass it on without symptoms.
We must cooperate in the shut downs despite impacts.

The ten happiest countries cooperate in disasters,
the ten unhappiest countries are torn apart by wars.
Pollution travels. Plasticized oceans effect us all.

California has shut down. Some folks are stir-crazy,
some create and innovate during their forced isolation.
Spring term courses are taught on-line. Lots of home-schoolers.

Some help their neighbors with groceries and other tasks.
Musicians play calming music for screens. Medical
supplies need increased producers and production.

Media updates progress and spread of the virus.
By washing our hands we'll clean up our act?
Togetherness less touchy-feely?

This sunny, warming Spring Equinox finds me
absorbing chi in a pillow-less chair in the backyard,
my only excursion outside. Inside my haven.

Wherever I plant myself, I'll observe and contemplate,
try to stay on track to find my highest path.
The quest, the curiosity spurs my greening.

Metamorphosis

Any transition serious enough to alter your definition of self will require not just small adjustments in your way of living and thinking but a full-on metamorphosis. Martha Beck

In the midst of self-quarantine in a pandemic
will this transition be serious enough to alter
humanity's definition of themselves?

Will the kindness, all-in-this-together mentality
transfer after the fear and danger lessens? Will
shut-downs, social distancing bring us closer soon?

As I sit in the backyard absorbing the sun
and looping chi with deep breaths, I observe
trees budding, flowers blooming, altering forms.

But as they change they remain innately
in their essence what they are supposed to be.
My body and mind contains my DNA code.

I will not be young and agile again, probably
not thinner either. Last stage of my metamorphosis?
Annuals and perennials seem to know their life paths.

Nature is not stagnant. The only constant is change.
As long as I am conscious and cogent, my core
adapts? I am uniquely me. My next transition death?

Am I to focus on the Now? As I shelter in place
I have plenty of time to contemplate changes and
create new dreams. I am cocooning.

Uneven Ground

Mid-March, mid-afternoon Hump Day
I venture into the backyard with my walker
to stabilize on uneven ground.

The legs of my chi chair sunk into scraggly grass.
I'm firmly implanted to survey bumpy, burgeoning
landscape and cloud-scattering sky.

A ghostly cloud splits and shifts amid clusters.
Skeletal shadows etch across the yard.
I see four dandelions- my beloved solar dots!

A small patch of tiny blue blooms with a white center
emerged under the apple tree. Lumpy fruit and nut trees
just have white niblets. Spiky lavender stalks may be lupin.

The lawn hosts remnant brown leaves, lichen twigs,
two of the dandelions. Blades broke free of recent
uniform butch-cut, sprawl with spring-green.

Tootsie, the weathervane angel remains stagnant
beside the pinwheel which wind spins languidly
and the wind-chimes barely jangle in the breeze.

Airlika, the rusty angel blows her silent horn from
the hazelnut limb above me. Bluebirds fly by.
A cat paws dirt near the neighbors' wire fence.

I experience emotional upheaval as I contemplate
postponing planned eye surgery amid the pandemic.
Uncertainty surrounds me, jarring my thoughts.

I deep breathe, huff and puff chi, then stand,
grab the walker to navigate uneven ground,
over patio stones, door mat to a flat slate floor.

Touching

It is touching to see the acts of kindness
during this coronavirus, non-touching time.
We are working together, stress what binds us.
We care, self-quarantine as the statistics climb.
> The elderly are at increased risk, also
> sales of hygiene products, briskly go.

During this coronavirus, non-touching time
stay six feet apart, don't touch your face,
wash your hands while singing, reciting a rhyme,
self-quarantine at home and in place.
> Rely on your screens to entertain?
> Stay-at-home children won't complain.

We are working together, stress what bind us.
Shop for others, take-out not sit in restaurants to feed.
Leave most all events and meetings behind us,
focus on others who are most in need.
> Give outside concerts from the street.
> Sing out windows, on porches–a treat.

We care, self-quarantine as the statistics climb.
We try to calm fears, increase testing capacity.
Hospital equipment needs are at a prime.
Our leadership lacks veracity.
> Increase production of essential goods,
> and stop stockpiling special foods.

The elderly are at increased risk, also
caring facilities breed viral spread.
Virus takes a deadly blow.
More elderly among the dead.
> Loneliness is also an serious issue.
> Paper products shortage and tissue.

Sales of hygiene products briskly go.
Stocks disappear as people hoard.
How long it'll last? Experts don't seem to know.
Everyone must get on board.
> Touch each other by the heart not hands.
> Follow protocols this virus demands.

240

Flattening the Curve
It is under the greatest adversity that there exists the greatest potential for doing good, both for oneself and others. Dalai Lama

Amid the greenth of a sunny spring day,
I sit inside social distancing, crossing out
events and meetings on my calendar.

Today we cancelled my 80th birthday dinner
as most restaurants are closed and I am
self-quarantined with hubby enforcement.

My planned eye surgery at the end of March
probably will get postponed as well.
I am a viral target trying to keep everyone safe.

I am trying to flatten to curve of viral spread.
It looks so lovely out while chaos swirls
in the pandemic fallout world-wide.

With industry and travel curbed, greenhouse
gases are reduced. China saw great declines.
Restrictions are imposed on us all.

In Spain residents cheered health workers
while Italians sang from their balconies.
People rely on each other, try to help.

Workers without income. Unschooled children
must have delivered food. Assisted living places
hard hit. Public places and gatherings shut down.

I can only do my bit. Flattening the curve
of infection is a goal, a dream...possible?
We are all in this together. Another challenge.

Social Distancing

Social
distancing can
be prudent, stressful and fun.
You call and email to keep
in touch.

Stockpile,
but do not hoard.
Avoid going to crowds.
So much is cancelled you will stay
at home.

When you
call someone they
are more likely to be
at home. Some are working at home
by choice.

But some
people lose income,
have no home and are cold,
vulnerable to corona
virus.

Six feet
apart. Don't touch
face or others, wash hands.
It's a time out. Pursue hobbies.
Relax.

Unknown
consequences
challenge sense of balance.
Elderly folks prematurely
can die.

I'll watch
comedies and
word-play, phone and email.
Watch screens for updates and wonder
if real?

Social Distancing Playing Scrabble

One of our Scrabble players suggested
playing Scrabble outside six feet apart.
It was a joke, but a fun challenge
to how this could be done.

We would have to go up to the board,
one at a time, place the tiles and return
to our socially distant seat. Be careful
to walk straight and not breathe near anyone.

We could take our turn, not knowing what
was put on the board. We would have to
place all the tiles, not touching for pick-up.
Maybe on another table to avoid contact?

All this would have to be carefully coordinated.
We would be within voice range. If we relied
on a smart phone, I would be in a pickle. I am
still learning. Might up my curve by necessity?

Some in the group play on-line with strangers.
One suggested we find a way to do so with
our group. I'm not the techie to figure it out.
I'll just take a hiatus from Scrabble for now.

My mother's name Honey appears in games
of Cooperative Scrabble. I hope she sees
from beyond we are not playing, so not excluding
her from our word-play. She watches anyhow?

Would we sanitize the tiles before and after
we play? Squirt the board with sanitizer? This
could be quite a project. Imaginative Scrabble
could be a real set-up, take down hazard.

Imagination can create new ways to play,
to conjure a world from our dreams. I will
word-play with other patterns, scrabble letters
and place them in new contexts in new games.

Dealing with Now

*You cannot find yourself in the past or future. The only place where you can find
yourself is in the Now.* Eckhart Tolle

Now finds us in the midst of a global pandemic,
social distancing, self-quarantine for who knows how long.
Debates and forecasts remain polemic.
Who knows how long this situation will prolong?
      People are isolated, anxious, out of touch.
      We cope while not knowing much.

Social distancing, self-quarantine for who knows how long.
Time to contemplate your soul and your navel?
Time to build awareness, become "woke", be strong?
Time to witness how circumstances unravel.
      Six feet apart, often washing your hands.
      Follow the protocols society demands.

Debates and forecasts remain polemic.
So much data is still unknown.
Root causes and treatments may be systemic.
How much responsibility will we own?
      Statistics become more important when you are one.
      How long will this pandemic run?

Who knows how long this situation will prolong?
It could become more deadly and wide-spread.
Will we face the challenge headlong?
So many living in fear and dread.
      Is this another global wake-up call,
      to steward planet better for us all?

People are isolated, anxious, out of touch.
Too few test kits, masks, protection aids.
Lack of leadership we can vouch.
We need accurate information that persuades
      everyone to heed medical advice.
      Everyone is asked to sacrifice.

We cope while not knowing much
about the current viral strain.
Any certainty we can clutch?
Living with stress will remain.
      Are we culling excess population?
      So many questions. Answers lack information.

Curtains

Curtains
closed to cold,
await opening warmth,
conceal burgeoning spring,
greening.

Curtains
await sun, some heat.
Rain streaks windows, snow melt,
dribbling down our fearful faces
and hearts.

Curtains
closed by the fact
we are in quarantine
from a pandemic, coronavirus
outbreak.

Curtains
will open when
warmer weather comes to
kill virus which likes it cold and
juicy.

Curtains
at my house peek
at sun rays, which can splay
across beds, invade busy rooms
to shine.

Curtains
to the virus,
globally infecting
spirits, covering uncertain
windows.

Playing Hooky

With the viral pandemic closing schools,
students can play hooky with permission.
Adults can play hooky by social distancing
as events and meetings cancel.

Whether self-imposed or forced, dropping
out of contact can be a vacation or
interruption of income. Time to find focus
or distraction through a turbulent time.

As people hermit, stockpile, reduce touching,
hand- washing and greeting rituals change.
Electrical devices and screens avoid
direct interaction. Playing hooky encouraged.

In high school my mother allowed me
to stay home to rest after a hectic week.
She even wrote an excuse, though I was
not sick, just exhausted. I was grateful.

Today as an old crone, a target for this virus,
I welcome some down time to catch up,
drop out of commotion. Phones and email
help me contact those I need to.

I'm cocooning at home, nurturing in place
until I can unfurl my wings and fly into spring.
Playing hooky rearranges things and lets
me re-assess what is important and how to act.

Friday the 13th 2020

We are in the midst of COVID-19 pandemic.
Seems we are all feeling somewhat unlucky.
The debates over data is mostly academic.
What we learn is increasingly yucky.
      Now we practice social distance.
      Now we isolate, quarantine for instance.

Seems we are all feeling somewhat unlucky.
We are left alone with our electronic devices.
Leaders' approaches appear mucky.
Hope our protective practice suffices.
      Everything's cancelled, shut down.
      It is quieter in our college town.

The debates over data is mostly academic.
False and inadequate "facts", lack of reliable sources.
Misinformation is endemic.
We are running out of supplies and resources.
      We must wash our hands, not touch our face.
      The virus attacks mostly elderly of every race.

What we learn is increasingly yucky.
Death toll climbs, but more die from the flu.
Will humanity rise to challenge, prove plucky?
Will we ever figure out what we must do?
      So many other issues need to be addressed.
      We are even more doubtful, weary and stressed.

Now we practice social distance,
if we are considerate and responsible.
Wearing masks faces some resistance.
Disregard makes contagion possible.
      Wash your hands singing "Happy Birthday" or
      time 20 seconds at least or more.

Now we isolate, quarantine for instance,
whether by self or by force.
We have to adjust to any circumstance.
We all should cooperate, of course.
      How many times do we have to fight
      and hope things will turn out right?

The Pep Talk

As the COVID-19 pandemic spreads fear,
experts and gurus urge us to be calm.
Some feel an extinction might be near.
Others say it will go away when its warm.
       Events, schools cancel, go on-line.
       News is wonky, says all will be fine.

Experts and gurus urge us to be calm.
Practice social distancing, wash your hands.
Hot drinks might be your balm.
Try to exercise reasonable demands.
       Maybe we touch too much?
       Invent new greetings and such?

Some feel an extinction might be near,
as the planet is polluted, poisoning air.
Now a cough, can contaminate the atmosphere.
Time to step up and become aware.
       This virus attacks mostly the sickly and old.
       Children and young adults less so we're told.

Some say it will go away when its warm.
China predicts by June, it is at its peak.
Not all die, but does economic harm.
Virus likes to prey on the weak.
       Air flights cancelled. Travel Greta's style.
       Our short term adjustments may last awhile

Events, schools cancel, go on-line.
Sports seasons shortened to protect fans.
Find something else to do in quarantine.
A time to reevaluate your plans.
       Fox News says it is all a hoax.
       "Fake news" standard for those folks.

News wonky, says all will be fine.
Often "fake news", says "stable genius" Trump.
Be mindful, get "woke", redefine.
This may be the chance to dump inept chump.
       World-wide it's time to be alert
       to prevent more from being hurt.

Update! COVID-19 Talk

> The Center for Global Health Oregon State University, *"COVID-19 Pandemic and its Global Impacts"* presented by epidemiologist Jeff Bettel and Professor Chunhai Chi

Each speaker will present for 15 minutes
followed by an open discussion.

In efforts to minimize the risk of spreading germs,
the forum will enact the following precautions.

All Kidder 202 windows will remain open
throughout the event, so dress accordingly.

All attendees need to write down their email
address so they can be contacted in the future
if necessary.

And a photo will be taken of the event
so we can map out where everyone
was sitting.

In addition, all attendees need to use
hand sanitizer prior to entering the room.

Space is limited, viewing via livestream
is encouraged. The livestream will be available
at live.oregonstate.edu.

The recorded video will be posted on the
college's YouTube channel after the event.

What if not everyone wanting to go received
this email? Same day, all classes went on-line
and most campus events cancelled.

Viral Fallout

The coronavirus is closing schools, public gatherings
and meetings. We went to see Women's Gymnastics
on March 6th. Oregon State vs University of Washington.
Sparser crowd. U of W closed classes to access on-line.

People who have recently visited Seattle, very leery.
As the virus spreads, so does the panic, as it is in the news.
People are not touching people, faces, washing hands.
Test have not proven effective. Hand wipes out at stores.

People are stocking up for expected isolation. My emails
are full of cancelled events, groups postponing meetings.
We even had a test county alert on phones and computers.
Apparently hot drinks and heat steer the virus elsewhere?

Charts and maps of the viral epidemic can be found on
pages and screens. The statistics show current progress,
numbers, countries, deaths. We have had viruses before.
Some flus more deadly. The planet faces many scourges.

Scientists have other concerns like asteroid strikes, cosmic
explosions, climate change, waste disposal, our space junk
orbit, forever chemicals, plastics, pollution, non-stable geniuses.
Many attacks on our vulnerable fleshy body and juicy planet.

For now I will drink hot tea, keep my hands under control,
keep up to date, stay grounded and won't fly, try to avoid
contamination. How many assaults can humans take
before we accept possible extinction or alien replacement?

Clamming Up

We are to maintain a social distance
of six feet and do not have face or hands
contact as the coronavirus goes viral.

A healthy, but anti-social circumstance.
Media makes sure everyone understands
new interactions, so disease won't spiral.

Crowds and coughs to be avoided.
Many sports events and meetings cancelled.
Stay home until the virus passes.

Masks and gloves by fear exploited.
Many greetings are repelled.
Be vigilant no one trespasses.

We are clamming up, retreating,
invent new ways for greeting.

Touching Faces

With coronavirus about, don't touch faces.
One virus can hitchhike into mouth, up nose.
No more greetings, facial embraces.
Invent other rituals, I suppose.
   One careless touch is a health risk.
   The spread in your body can be brisk.

One virus can hitchhike into mouth, up nose,
can cause lung and kidney damage, quite lethal
septic shock, organ failure, breathing can close.
Sometimes the virus can be fatal.
   Face touching helps us deal with anxiety,
   and distraction. Enforce healthy propriety.

No more greetings, facial embraces,
to increase dangers of contamination.
Virus infects, while hand-washing erases
some of the contacts in a situation.
   Colonies of bacteria found on phones.
   Tends to effect geezers and crones.

Invent other rituals I suppose,
wave, hit elbows, knees, wear gloves,
some cultures greet with toes.
Many use hand-sanitizers, avoid droves,
   stay home as events and schools cancel,
   anywhere large crowds and virus dwell.

One careless touch is a health risk.
Be mindful, fold busy hands, don't itch,
gloves discourage touching face and screens. Don't frisk.
Use tongue depressor if itchy. Listen to pitch
   to wash hands often. Try not to touch faces.
   Avoid contaminated places.

The spread in your body can be brisk.
Learn symptoms and seek medical attention.
Will your life become an asterisk?
Can you follow through your best intention?
   We have had many viruses before.
   Scientists predict we'll have many more.

Manifesting My Cloister

During my confinement, I am not alone.
My husband and I perfect our routines
and modify our confines to suit us.

My seasonal decorations have shifted
for the duration of the pandemic perhaps,
since the next change is Halloween.

I notice each miniature at different times
focusing in on their details and how they
became a part of my life. I love color and texture.

Many "experts" advise using candles,
flowers, get a pet to spark things up.
I use what I have now. Avoid going out.

My husband made a mask of a tee-shirt
sleeve and paper insert. People are so
clever with fabrics and design.

Since I do not plan to go out for weeks
and have been home for weeks, no masks
no gloves, just hand-washing.

I chose Danish "hygge", making home
comfortable over Finnish "pantsdrunk"
getting drunk in underwear.

My calendar is full of crossed out
meetings, appointments and events.
I am content writing, perusing screens.

My cloister may not be totally spiritual,
more mundane, but taking a deep breath
and praying is a response to the turbulence.

Skyview

During this pandemic, when so many
people stay home, don't travel, don't go to work,
satellite images show less pollution. Any
ideas how to connect, form a new network?
      Birds migrate north this late spring.
      Planes fly less which is a blessing.

People stay home, don't travel, don't go to work.
Caved indoors they do not see clearing sky.
Some are fearful they will go berserk.
Too many unanswered questions as to why
      virus droplets float in the air.
      So many people remain unaware.

Satellite images show less pollution, any
progress with reduction may not last.
This virus is mysterious and uncanny.
It continues to spread globally and fast.
      The sky without its gritty bits,
      now carries unseen virus hits.

Ideas how to connect, form a new network,
create more air waves, add to the "Cloud",
innovation could provide another air perk,
instead of thickening a shroud.
      Rain cleanses, sun warms.
      Weather helps and harms.

Birds migrate north late this spring
flying long distances with less gunk in air.
Harbingers of spring, hopefully bring
a better climate, end of virus everywhere.
      Birds socially distance in our backyard.
      Mostly land solo. Their journey's hard.

Planes fly less which is a blessing.
They carry contagion and release pollution.
Many of their victims are convalescing,
while others await a vaccine solution.
      The sky surrounds us from vast space.
      The sky holds the future of the human race.

Living Vicariously

Normally, my husband Court and I
grocery shop separately- he, to healthy
First Alternative and Fred Meyer.

I zip on a red scooter at Safeway
plucking easy-to-prepare meals
and dark chocolate.

For the first time we called in
our order to Fred Meyer for pick up.
Our pick-up time was a week later.

First he rambled in uncrowded
First Alternative, filling little bags
with tiny pellets of organic fare.

Then Fred Meyer. They have six
pick up slots. When you arrive at
your time, you call in to tell them.

Only two cars there and few in
the parking lot. Court was masked
and gloved. The food carrier was not.

He did not need the boxes he brought,
as there were plenty of paper bags.
When he unloaded, after a shower

and clothes change, I watched the
unveiling and checked the grocery list.
Everything we ordered was there.

I miss my scooter, seeing people in
person, not on page or screen. Our
mutual groceries un-bag, separate.

How long until we shop normally?
When will I stop self-quarantine
with my own delivery man?

My Staycation

I am sheltering in place, social
distancing, washing hands,
staying in self-quarantine.

I am trying to view the situation
as a vacation, a time to relax,
free creativity, contact without touch.

All the isolating terms due to the
coronavirus renew worries, fears
for others, feel sadly heavy-handed.

But in my green oasis, I can soak
in intermittent sun, escape screens
when I can no longer take dark barrage.

I can only sign so many petitions, endure
so much news, tolerate misguiding leadership
just so long until I go on staycation mode.

Some solace comes with solitude,
reducing exposure to media's manipulation.
There are no meetings or events to go to.

My mindset is to remind myself I am retired,
elderly. It's my time to create what I choose.
I'll help others if I can. But I'm on staycation.

Other Poetry Books by Linda Varsell Smith

Cinqueries: A Cluster of Cinquos and Lanterns
Fibs and Other Truths
Black Stars on a White Sky
Poems That Count
Poems That Count Too
* Winging-It: New and Selected Poems
*Red Cape Capers: Playful Backyard Meditations
*Star Stuff: A Soul-Splinter Experiences the Cosmos
*Light-Headed: A Soul-Splinter Experiences Light
* Sparks: A Soul-Splinter Experiences Earth
* Into the Clouds: Seeking Silver Linings
*Mirabilia: Manifesting Marvels, Miracles and Mysteries
*Spiral Hands: Signs of Healing
*Lacunae: Mind the Gap
*Wayfinding: Navigating the Unknown
* Wordy-Smith: Dancing the Line
* Hugger-Muggery:Ways to Hugs and Mugs
* The Ground Crew: Beings with Earthly Experiences
* Waves: Ebbs and Flows
* Grounded With Gaia: Bonded with Earth

* Available at www.Lulu.com/spotlight/rainbowcom

Chapbooks

Being Cosmic, Intra-space Chronicles,
Light-Headed, Red Cape Capers

On-Line Web-site Books on Poetry Forms

Free-access @ RainbowComunications.org
Syllables of Velvet   Word-Playful   Poetluck

Anthologies

The Second Genesis, Branches, Poetic License,
Poetic License 2015, Jubilee, The Eloquent Umbrella

Twelve novels in the Rainbow Chronicles Series